Terrestrial Vegetation and Soils Monitoring in Coronado National Memorial, 2009–2010

Natural Resource Data Summary NPS/SODN/NRDS—2011/215

Authors

J. Andrew Hubbard
Sarah E. Studd
Sonoran Desert Network
National Park Service
7660 E. Broadway Blvd., #303
Tucson, AZ 85710

Cheryl L. McIntyre
New Mexico State University
Water Resources Research Institute
MSC 3167
PO Box 30001
Las Cruces, NM 88003

Editing and Design

Alice Wondrak Biel
Sonoran Desert Network
National Park Service
7660 E. Broadway Blvd., #303
Tucson, AZ 85710

December 2011

U.S. Department of the Interior
National Park Service
Natural Resource Stewardship and Science
Fort Collins, Colorado

The National Park Service, Natural Resource Stewardship and Science office in Fort Collins, Colorado publishes a range of reports that address natural resource topics of interest and applicability to a broad audience in the National Park Service and others in natural resource management, including scientists, conservation and environmental constituencies, and the public.

The Natural Resource Data Series is intended for timely release of basic data sets and data summaries. Care has been taken to assure accuracy of raw data values, but a thorough analysis and interpretation of the data has not been completed. Consequently, the initial analyses of data in this report are provisional and subject to change.

All manuscripts in the series receive the appropriate level of peer review to ensure that the information is scientifically credible, technically accurate, appropriately written for the intended audience, and designed and published in a professional manner. This report received informal peer review by subject-matter experts who were not directly involved in the collection, analysis, or reporting of the data.

This report is available from the Sonoran Desert Network website, http://www.nature.nps.gov/im/units/sodn/, as well as at the Natural Resource Publications Management web site, http://www.nature.nps.gov/publications/nrpm/.

Please cite this publication as:

Hubbard, J. A., C. L. McIntyre, and S. E. Studd. 2011. Terrestrial vegetation and soils monitoring in Coronado National Memorial, 2009–2010. Natural Resource Data Series NPS/SODN/NRDS—2011/215. National Park Service, Fort Collins, Colorado.

NPS 401/111798, December 2011

Contents

Figures

Tables

Main Report

Appendices

Executive Summary

This report summarizes data of the Sonoran Desert Network's first two seasons of terrestrial vegetation and soils monitoring in upland areas of Coronado National Memorial, in southern Arizona. Twelve permanent monitoring sites were sampled, with another 19 planned for 2011–2013, after which time a detailed status and trend report will be produced. The current report summarizes effort to date, evaluates the sampling design in the context of our monitoring objectives, and suggests modifications to the design.

Based on estimates from this initial data, the design does an effective job of providing statistical power to detect trends for most perennial species, lifeforms, and soil parameters. However, the erratic abundance (including some of the highest cover values we've ever measured for any species) of Lehmann lovegrass (*Eragrostis lehmanniana*), a problematic non-native invasive grass, presents a challenge for efficient trend detection. Species detectability appears to be very reasonable based on species-accumulation curves. Although only about 19% of the known park flora have been detected to date, the protocol does not call for differentiating among annuals (with the exception of exotic plants), nor for sampling aquatic, riparian, or xeroriparian systems. Additionally, only about one-third of the planned plots have been sampled to date.

The elevation × soil texture stratification scheme is difficult to assess at this time. There were few significant differences in vegetation communities of the four strata, with the exception of those found in low-elevation, non-rocky soils as compared to mid-elevation, very to extremely rocky soils and rock outcrops. This lack of differentiation between strata is likely due to the small sample sizes of these more constrained areas of the park, although sampling efficiencies can be gained if the lack of differences is found to be real. We will investigate this question by adding one site at high elevation in 2011, and by shifting the sampling schedule for the other small strata forward to 2011. Results will be analyzed in the 2011 data summary. Evaluating and (if warranted) modifying the stratification scheme is the best approach for resolving power issues, as well.

Overall, the sampling and response designs are efficient and effective, and should provide data that meet our monitoring objectives. We will continue to evaluate and adjust our sampling strategy annually, culminating in the full analysis for a comprehensive status and trend report after the 2013 season. Therefore, it is important that results in this and other annual data summaries not be directly interpreted for evaluating the condition of park resources.

Acronyms

ANOSIM	analysis of similarity
AVG	average
GRTS	generalized random tessellation stratified
MDC	minimum detectable change
MDS	non-metric multi-dimensional scaling
n	number
NMEM	national memorial
NPS	National Park Service
P	probability of obtaining a test statistic equal to observed when null hypothesis is true (=no differences)
R	similarity index in which 0 = exactly the same, 1 = completely dissimilar
RRQRR	reversed randomized quadrant recursive raster
SD	standard deviation
Sdiff	standard deviation of the differences
SE	standard error
SODN	Sonoran Desert Network

Acknowledgements

We thank former superintendent Kym Hall, Chief of Resources Danielle Foster, and the staff and volunteers of Coronado National Memorial for their on-site support of this field effort and the Sonoran Desert Network Inventory & Monitoring Program (SODN). Beth Fallon, Laura Crumbacher, Zach Ahrens, David Fenlon, Greg Goodrum, Stephanie Roussel, Kate Connor, Betsy Vance, Dan Stauning, Laura Tennant, and Steve Buckley conducted the field-data collection. Betsy Vance tirelessly processed the soil samples. Expert data processing and management was completed by SODN Data Manager Kristen Beaupré, and Laura Crumbacher updated the master plant lists.

1 Introduction

1.1 Background

Generating more than 99.9% of Earth's biomass (Whittaker 1975), plants are the primary producers of life on our planet. Vegetation therefore represents much of the biological foundation of terrestrial ecosystems, and it comprises or interacts with all primary structural and functional components of these systems. Vegetation dynamics can indicate the integrity of ecological processes, productivity trends, and ecosystem interactions that can otherwise be difficult to monitor. Land management actions often focus on manipulating vegetation to achieve park management objectives, with defined conditions based on community structure or lifeform composition.

In the Sonoran Desert and Apache Highlands ecoregions (Bailey 1998), vegetation composition, distribution, and production are highly influenced by edaphic factors, such as soil texture, mineralogy depth, and landform type (McAuliffe 1999). Especially as they relate to water, these influences are magnified at local scales, as described by pioneering desert ecologist Forrest Shreve:

> The profound influence of soil upon desert vegetation is to be attributed to its strong control of the amount, availability and continuity of water supply. This fundamental requisite in plants is the most effective single factor in the differentiation of desert communities (Shreve 1951).

As such, a fundamental understanding of soils and landforms is essential for evaluating vegetation patterns and processes (McAuliffe 1999).

The Sonoran Desert Network (SODN), as part of the National Park Service's Inventory and Monitoring Program, has identified terrestrial vegetation and dynamic soil functional attributes as important ecosystem monitoring parameters or "vital signs" (NPS 2005) that provide key insights into the integrity of terrestrial ecosystems at Coronado National Memorial (NMEM; Figure 1-1). Indicators of terrestrial vegetation integrity include vegetation community structure, lifeform abundance, status and trends of established exotic plants, and early detection of previously undetected exotic plants. Indicators of soil dynamic function and erosion resistance include the cover of mineral soil, the stability of surface soil aggregates, and the abundance of biological soil crusts.

1.2 Goals and objectives

The overall goal of the SODN terrestrial vegetation and soils monitoring program is to ascertain broad-scale changes in vegetation and dynamic soils properties in the context of changes in other ecological drivers, stressors, processes, and focal resources of interest. This integrated approach explores patterns and identifies candidate explanations to support effective management and protection of park natural resources in a cumulative fashion, such that the results of each successive round of monitoring build upon the knowledge gained from previous efforts and related research and monitoring activities.

Specific, measurable objectives for SODN terrestrial vegetation and soils monitoring (Hubbard et al. in review) at Coronado NMEM are to determine the status of and detect trends in (over 5-year intervals):

1. Terrestrial *vegetation cover* for common (≥10% absolute canopy cover) perennial species, including non-native plants, and all plant lifeforms.

2. Terrestrial *vegetation frequency* of uncommon (<10% absolute canopy cover) perennial species, including non-native plants.

3. Terrestrial *soil cover* by substrate classes (bare soil, litter, vegetation, biological soil crust, rock fragments of several size classes) that influence resistance to erosion.

4. Terrestrial *soil stability* of surface aggregates by stability class (1–6).

5. *Basal cover* of biological soil crusts by morphological group.

1.3 Scope of this report

This document summarizes the results of the first two years of terrestrial vegetation and soils monitoring in Coronado National Memorial. As Coronado NMEM is a relatively large park with challenging and diverse topography, we employ a multi-year sampling strategy in which one-fifth of the monitoring sites are sampled in a given year, with the entire complement completed after five field seasons (i.e., in 2013). Therefore, only two-fifths of the sampling has occurred to date, and we do not synthesize and interpret the current information in the context of status or trends. Instead, the objectives of this report are to:

- Document the processed data from the first two years of this multi-year effort.

- Evaluate the stratification approach and sample sizes based on vegetation similarity, estimated statistical power, and species detectability.

- If warranted by the data, adjust strata and sample sizes to ensure we are meeting the monitoring objectives.

It is therefore critical that the reader not draw overall conclusions based on this report alone.

We will continue to produce annual data summaries and refine the sampling design as necessary, with a much more detailed and comprehensive synthesis report to be created after the final complement of sampling in 2013. For an example of a final status and trend report, see Terrestrial Vegetation and Soils Monitoring at Fort Bowie National Historic Site: 2008 Status Report (Hubbard et al. 2010), available at http://science.nature. nps.gov/im/units/sodn/docs/AR_FOBO_Uplands_2009.pdf.

The thematic scope of this report is limited to terrestrial ecosystems. Aquatic resources, including riparian and xeroriparian vegetation, are addressed in SODN protocols for monitoring Washes and Seeps, Springs, and Tinajas.

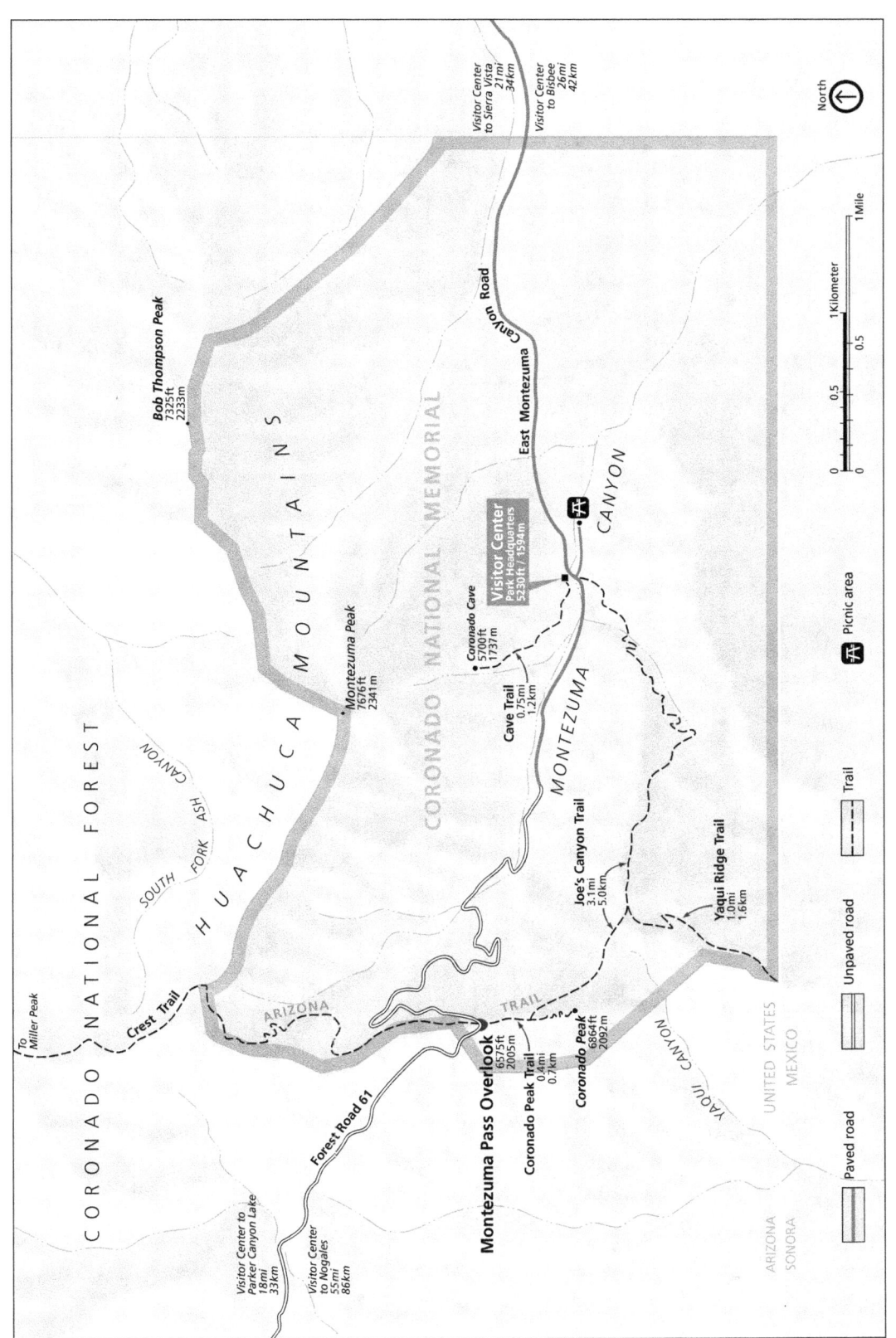

Figure 1-1. Coronado National Memorial.

2 Methods

2.1 Response design

The response design for this protocol employs permanent, 20 × 50-m sampling plots (Figure 2-1). The 50-m edges of the plot run parallel with the contours of the site. Vegetation sampling is performed, in conjunction with soil cover and stability measures, along six transects within each plot. In the spaces between transects (subplots), within-plot frequency is estimated by noting the occurrence of any plant species or lifeform not observed on the adjacent transects. See Hubbard and others (in review) for details on plot configuration and data collection.

2.1.1 Vegetation, biological soil crust, and soil cover: Line-point intercept

Line-point intercept is a common and efficient technique for measuring the vegetation cover of plants. Line-point intercept measures the number of "hits" of a given species out of the total number of points measured (Elzinga et al. 1998; Bonham 1989). Vegetation was recorded within three height categories along each of the six transects using the line-point intercept method, with points spaced every 0.5 m (240 points total). The three height categories were field (<0.5 m), subcanopy (0.5–2.0 m), and canopy (>2.0 m) (Table 2-1). Perennial vegetation was recorded to species and annual vegetation was recorded to lifeform, with the exception of a suite of annual non-native plants that were recorded to the species level. Soil cover (see Hubbard et al. in review, SOP #4) was recorded by substrate class (e.g., rock, gravel, litter), with biological soil crust cover recorded to morphological group (e.g., light cyanobacteria, dark cyanobacteria, lichen, moss).

Table 2-1. Height categories for vegetation measurement.

Layer	Height
Field	<0.5 m
Subcanopy	0.5–2.0 m
Canopy	>2.0 m

2.1.2 Vegetation frequency: Subplots

The area between any two adjacent transects formed the boundary of 10 × 20-m subplots that were used to estimate within-plot frequency of perennial plant species, exotic plants, and all lifeforms. The occurrence of any species/lifeform not measured on the adjacent line-point transect was recorded to determine a within-plot frequency of 0–5. Figure 2-1 explains the relationship between each subplot and its corresponding adjacent transect.

2.1.3 Soil aggregate stability

Surface soil aggregate stability was measured using a modified wet aggregate stability method (Herrick et al. 2005a). Within each plot, samples were attempted at 48 pre-determined points on either side of the six line-point intercept transects. A total of uniformly sized (2–3 mm thick and 6–8 mm on each side) samples were tested per plot, in groups of 16. Each sample was placed on a screen and soaked in water for five minutes. After five minutes, the samples were slowly dipped up and down in the water, with the remaining amount of soil recorded as an index of the wet aggregate stability of the sample. Samples were scored from 1 to 6, with 6 being the most stable.

2.1.4 Soil and site characterization

Proximate soil and landform factors are known to influence vegetation and dynamic soil function parameters at local scales (McAuliffe 1999). To characterize the soil and landscape attributes of each plot, a suite of topoedaphic variables was collected through site diagrams, repeat photo points, and collection of soil cores. Landform, slope position, and parent material were recorded at each plot. Flow–length diagrams were used to depict surface flow patterns and document the slopes (%) and lengths (m) of the hillslope within and immediately upslope of each plot. Permanent photo points were established at each plot corner to characterize general site physiognomy and as an aid to interpreting quantitative trend data in successive sampling periods. In addition, general site descriptions (including observed disturbances such as fire) were collected for each plot.

2.2 Sampling design

2.2.1 Overview

We allocated a total of 30 permanent monitoring plots in a spatially balanced arrangement (see Section 2.2.3), based on a priori expectations of required sample size to meet our criteria for statistical power and detectability (see Sections 2.2.5–2.2.6). Terrestrial vegetation and soils plots were

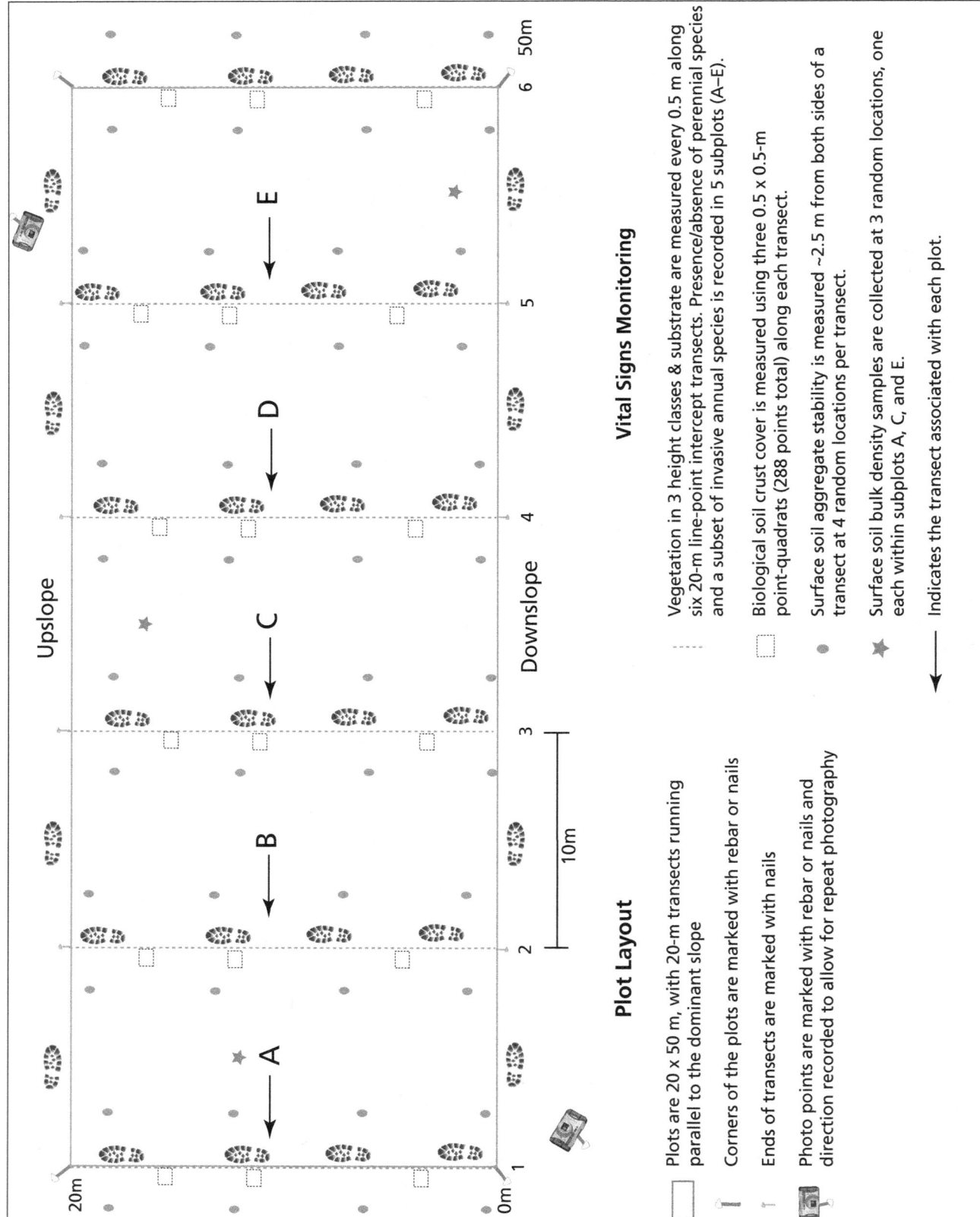

Plot Layout

☐ Plots are 20 x 50 m, with 20-m transects running parallel to the dominant slope

Corners of the plots are marked with rebar or nails

Ends of transects are marked with nails

Photo points are marked with rebar or nails and direction recorded to allow for repeat photography

Vital Signs Monitoring

- - - Vegetation in 3 height classes & substrate are measured every 0.5 m along six 20-m line-point intercept transects. Presence/absence of perennial species and a subset of invasive annual species is recorded in 5 subplots (A–E).

☐ Biological soil crust cover is measured using three 0.5 x 0.5-m point-quadrats (288 points total) along each transect.

● Surface soil aggregate stability is measured ~2.5 m from both sides of a transect at 4 random locations per transect.

★ Surface soil bulk density samples are collected at 3 random locations, one each within subplots A, C, and E.

→ Indicates the transect associated with each plot.

Figure 2-1. Terrestrial vegetation and soils monitoring plot design. See Hubbard et al. (in review) for additional details on design and data collection.

Table 2-2. Allocation of permanent terrestrial vegetation and soils monitoring plots by strata, Coronado National Memorial.

Stratum	Elevation	% rock fragments	Total area (acres)	Percentage of total		Plots per stratum	
				Park area	Frame area	Number (min. 3)	Number per year
Excluded			1,971	41	0	0	0
401	4,501–6,000'	<35%	331	7	12	4	1 or 0
402	4,501–6,000'	35–90%	1,183	25	42	13	2 or 3
403	4,501–6,000'	BRO	45	1	2	0	0
501	>6,000'	<35%	0.2	0	0	0	0
502	>6,000'	35–90%	994	21	35	10	2
503	>6,000'	BRO	292	6	10	3	1 or 0

BRO = bedrock or rock outcrops
Strata with <5% of park area (shown in grey) were excluded.

proportionately allocated to four strata based on elevation and soil type (Table 2-2, Figure 2-2). Stratification (see Section 3.2.2, Hubbard et al. in review) was employed to reduce spatial variability and increase sampling efficiency. Consequently, inference from the plots at Coronado NMEM is to all terrestrial areas of the park by elevation × soil strata, except for the areas discussed in Section 2.2.4.

2.2.2 Annual sampling

Permanent plots are employed to increase our ability to efficiently detect trends, by explicitly partitioning spatial and temporal variability (Elzinga et al. 1998). As with all designs, there are inherent tradeoffs with using permanent plots, as discussed in Hubbard and others (in review). The primary disadvantage at larger units (such as Coronado NMEM) is that sampling across landscapes (space) is reduced as field effort is dedicated to revisiting existing plots.

To ensure adequate spatial coverage, we employ a simple rotating panel design (McDonald 2003)

that allocates plots annually, such that each plot is revisited every five years [1,4], in line with our assumptions regarding the timing of biologically meaningful change (Hubbard et al. in review). Using this approach, the total population of plots in a park is apportioned evenly per year. For Coronado NMEM, the total anticipated sample size is 30 plots; therefore, approximately six plots are sampled each year (Table 2-3).

The advantages of this design are that (1) the influence of interannual variation (i.e., noise) is less pronounced for the analysis of five-year trends; and (2) there are tremendous efficiency gains, from the perspective of fielding and funding sampling crews, as effort is spread evenly over five-year intervals. The disadvantages are that (1) the effects of individual stochastic events may be difficult to evaluate (Hubbard et al. in review) and (2) detecting trends requires at least 10 years of data collection (i.e., two sampling intervals for all plots). Rotating-panel designs generally allow trend detection over shorter time periods (particularly when a subset of the plots is monitored continually), but sampling intensity is unlikely to

Table 2-3. Sampling schedule for Coronado National Memorial.

Stratum	Plots sampled		Plots not yet sampled		
	2009	2010	2011	2012	2013
401 (non-rocky soils, 4,501–6,000')	1	2	3	4	
402 (rocky soils, 4,501–6,000')	1, 2	3, 4	5, 6, 7	8, 9, 10	11, 12, 13
502 (rocky soils, >6,000')	3, 4	5, 8	9, 10	11, 12	13, 14
503 (bedrock or rock outcrops, >6,000')	1	6	-	-	8

Values are the site labels within each stratum. Adjustments within and between strata may occur based on early results. Section 2.2.2 describes the stratification scheme.

Vegetation & Soils Monitoring Plots

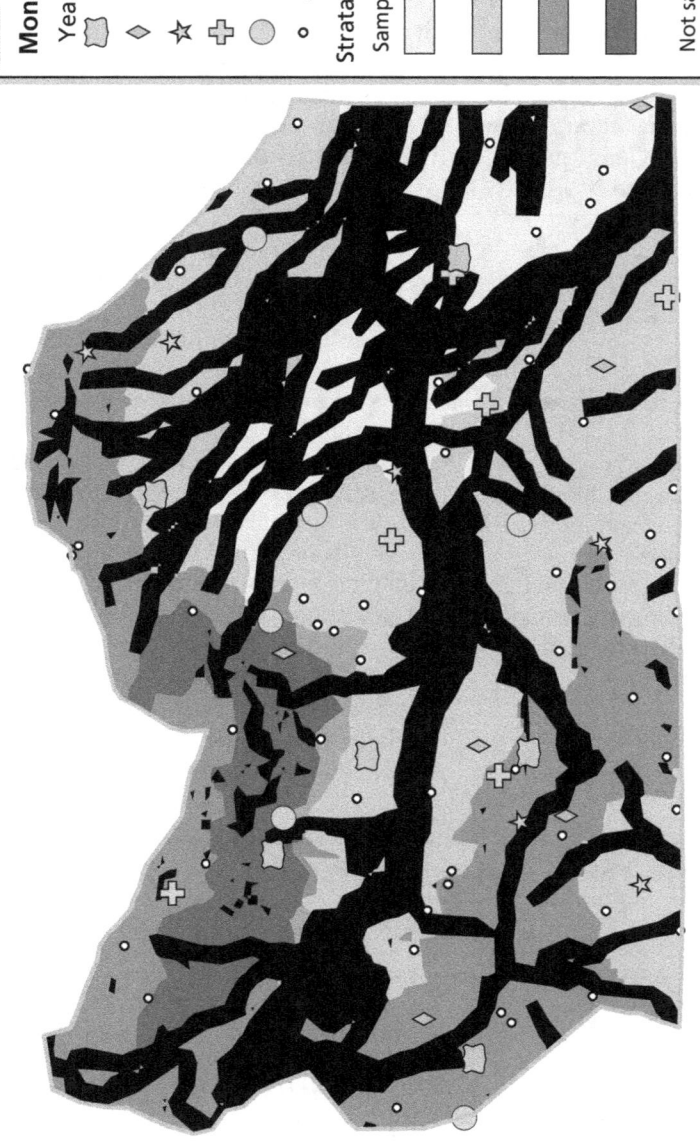

Legend

Legal boundary

Monitoring plots

Year of first visit

- 2009
- 2010
- 2011 (planned)
- 2012 (planned)
- 2013 (planned)
- Alternate

Strata/Number of plots

Sampled

- 401 (4,501–6,000'; <35% rock fragments/4 plots)
- 402 (4,501–6,000'; 35–90% rock fragments/13 plots)
- 502 (>6,000'; 35–90% rock fragments/10 plots)
- 503 (>6,000'; bedrock or rock outcrops/3 plots)

Not sampled

- Excluded (roads, trails, washes/0 plots)
- 403 (4,501–6,000'; bedrock or rock outcrops/0 plots)
- 501 (>6,000'; <35% rock fragments/0 plots)

September 2011

0 250 500 1,000 1,500 2,000 Meters

Produced by Sonoran Desert Network

Figure 2-2. Distribution of terrestrial vegetation and soils monitoring plots at Coronado NMEM.

meet our statistical-power and species-detection goals (see Sections 2.5–2.6). We ruled out intensive annual monitoring of a subset of plots due to concerns over plot degradation, as discussed in the SODN natural and cultural resource compliance effort (NPS 2005b).

If a major disturbance (e.g., fire, extended periods of temperature extremes, mass soil movement) occurs in the intervening years, we may collect additional plot data to characterize and account for the potential effects of these important stochastic events. For instance, at the time of this writing, the Monument fire had just occurred throughout much of the park. As a result, we will work with park staff to determine if additional plots (from the RRQRR ordered list) should be added to help us understand the implications of this important event. Any additional data will be reported in future data summary and status and trend reports.

2.2.3 Spatial balance

The spatial sampling design for this protocol employs permanent, 20 × 50-m sampling plots, allocated through a Reversed Randomized Quadrant-Recursive Raster (RRQRR) spatially balanced design (Theobald et al. 2007), using the "spatially balanced sample" function in the STARMAP Spatial Sampling Toolbox in ArcGIS 9.0 (http://www.spatialecology.com/htools/index.php). This tool produces a design that is spatially well-balanced, probability-based, flexible, and simple (Theobald et al. 2007). Because it tries to maximize the spatial independence between plots, the spatially-balanced sampling design should provide more information per plot, thus increasing efficiency (Theobald et al. 2007).

Spatially balanced designs, such as RRQRR (for polygon data) and the Generalized Random Tessellation Stratified (GRTS; for points and lines) approach (Stevens and Olsen 2004), are increasingly being applied to ecosystem monitoring (e.g., Environmental Protection Agency Ecological Monitoring and Assessment Program) because they provide the advantages of a probabilistic design (Stehman 1999) and ensure spatial balance regardless of overall sample size. RRQRR designs facilitate adding or removing sites in a spatially balanced manner if statistical power, financial considerations, or additional monitoring objectives warrant adjusting the sample size. This scaling ability is an important advantage, as (1) the number of plots per park cannot always be

adequately estimated a priori (see Section 3.4.2, Hubbard et al. in review) and (2) future changes in technology, objectives, and budgets may necessitate increasing or decreasing sample sizes.

2.2.4 Sampling frame

The sampling frame for Coronado NMEM includes all terrestrial areas within park boundaries, except for the following (Figure 2-2):

- Slopes of ≥45° (for crew safety)

- Roads and buildings (including 100-m buffer)

- Trails, washes, and streams (including 50-m buffer)

- Areas deemed unsafe due to illegal border activity

The total area excluded under these criteria was 1.971 acres (~797 ha), or 41% of the park area.

2.2.5 Management assessment points as the link between science and management

To achieve the National Park Service's core mission of resource protection, resource management and monitoring must be explicitly linked (Bingham et al. 2007). We advocate the use of management assessment points as a bridge between science and management. Management assessment points are "pre-selected points along a continuum of resource-indicator values where scientists and managers have agreed to stop and assess the status or trend of a resource relative to program goals, natural variation, or potential concerns" (Bennetts et al. 2007).

Management assessment points therefore aid interpretation of ecological information within a management context. They do not define strict management or ecological thresholds, inevitably result in management actions, or reflect any legal or regulatory standard; they are only intended to serve as a potential early warning system allowing scientists and managers to pause, review the available information in detail, and consider options. Bennetts and others (2007) provided a detailed explanation of this concept and its application to monitoring and management of protected areas.

Although no management assessment points have been formally established for Coronado NMEM, we intend to work with park staff to develop initial assessment points relevant to terrestrial vegetation and soils. For an example of the application of management assessment points, see Terrestrial Vegetation and Soils Monitoring at Fort Bowie National Historic Site: 2008 Status Report (Hubbard et al. 2010), available at: http://science.nature.nps.gov/im/units/sodn/docs/AR_FOBO_Uplands_2009.pdf.

2.2.6 Statistical power to distinguish status from management assessment points

Estimating our statistical power to distinguish current conditions (i.e., status) from management assessment points (see previous section) is important for both protocol design (especially for determining adequate sample sizes) and data interpretation. Adequate sample size (number of plots) is estimated by (Herrick et al. 2005b):

$$n = \frac{(S)^2 (Z_\alpha + Z_\beta)^2}{(MDC)^2}$$

Where:
- S = standard deviation of the sample,

- Z_α = Z-coefficient for false change (Type I) error (we set at 90%),

- Z_β = Z-coefficient for missed-change (Type II) error (we set at 10%), and

MDC = minimum detectable change size between time 1 and time 2 (set at 5–20%).

Bonham (1989), Elzinga and others (1998), and Herrick and others (2005b) provide detailed discussions of statistical power to detect differences from a standard.

2.2.7 Statistical power to detect trends

Statistical power is also important for evaluating trends (change over time) in monitoring parameters. Adequate sample size (number of plots) for detecting a trend of a given size across a landscape with permanent plots is estimated from:

$$n = \frac{(S_{diff})^2 (Z_\alpha + Z_\beta)^2}{(MDC)^2}$$

Where:
- S_{diff} = Standard deviation of the differences between paired samples,

- Z_α = Z-coefficient for false change (Type I) error (we set at 90%),

- Z_β = Z-coefficient for missed-change (Type II) error (we set at 10%), and

- MDC = minimum detectable change size between time 1 and time 2 (set at 5–20%).

Because we only have one sampling interval for this report, we estimated "S_{diff}" using the following equation:

$$S_{diff} = (S_1)(\sqrt{2(1 - corr_{diff})})$$

Where:

- S_1 = Sample standard deviation among sampling units at first time period, and

- $corr_{diff}$ = estimated correlation coefficient between time 1 and time 2, set at 0.75.

Bonham (1989), Elzinga and others (1998), and Herrick and others (2005b) provide detailed discussions of statistical power to detect trend.

2.2.8 Evaluation of strata

The terrestrial vegetation monitoring design apportions long-term monitoring sites to strata to improve the efficiency of parkwide estimation of monitoring parameters of interest. It is assumed that vegetation and dynamic soil functional attributes respond differently to environmental factors that can be clearly defined and are immutable over management and monitoring timescales (Bonham 1989).

To evaluate the efficiency and pertinence of our preselected elevation strata, we contrasted the similarity of the vegetation communities on each stratum using Analysis of Similarity (ANOSIM) and non-metric multidimensional scaling (NMDS), non-parametric, multivariate community analysis techniques that make few assumptions about the data, yielding a simple yet powerful analysis tool (Clarke and Warwick 2001).

3 Results

3.1 Vegetation monitoring

3.1.1 Species richness and distribution by height class

The field layer had the highest vegetation cover (68.5 ± 2.5%) and species richness (72 perennial species). The subcanopy layer had roughly half the cover and 60% of the perennial species (33.9 ± 3.1%, and 43, respectively) of the field layer. The canopy layer contained only 11.9 ± 4% cover from just eight species, reflecting the short-statured nature of these semiarid plant communities. No new species were detected during sampling.

3.1.2 Invasive exotic plants

Two invasive exotic plant species were detected on line-point transects: Lehmann lovegrass (*Eragrostis lehmanniana*), a bunchgrass, was found on the transects of seven plots and detected in the frequency subplots on an additional two plots (75% landscape frequency). Redstar (*Ipomea coccinea*), a vine, was found on the transects of two plots and detected in the frequency subplots on one additional plot (25% landscape frequency). The *I. coccinea* was found on very to extremely rocky sites. In addition, spreading fanpetals (*Sida abutifolia*), a forb, was detected on frequency subplots on 17% of the sites.

3.2 Evaluation of strata

For canopy-layer vegetation, Analysis of Similarity (ANOSIM) did not reveal any significant differences in plant communities ($P = 25.9\%$) between any of the four strata (Table 3-1). However, non-metric multidimensional scaling (MDS; Figure 3-1a) suggested that several plots contained localized, site-specific vegetation (similarity <20% with any other plot), including both plots at low-elevation, non-rocky soil sites (plots 402_V01, 402_V02), and one low-elevation, rocky site (402_V04).

For subcanopy and, especially, field-layer vegetation, both ANOSIM and MDS detected substantial structuring by strata. Field and subcanopy vegetation differed ($P \leq 6.7\%$) between rocky sites above 6,000' in elevation (502 stratum) and all plots below 6,000' (strata 401, 402), regardless of soil type (Table 3-1a, b). Interestingly, bedrock/rock outcrop sites above 6,000' (503 stratum) did

Table 3-1. Analysis of similarity (ANOSIM) results for pairwise tests contrasting vegetation composition by strata for (a) field, (b) subcanopy, and (c) canopy height classes for terrestrial vegetation monitoring at Coronado NMEM, 2009–2010.

a. Field (<0.5 m)
Global R: 0.508, $P = 1.2\%$

Groups	R	P
401 vs. 402	0.536	13.3%
401 vs. 502	1	**6.7%**
401 vs. 503	1	33.3%
402 vs. 502	0.302	**2.9%**
402 vs. 503	0.179	33.3%
502 vs. 503	0.25	20.0%

b. Subcanopy (0.5–2.0 m)
Global R: 0.448, $P = 1.2\%$

Groups	R	P
401 vs. 402	0.536	13.3%
401 vs. 502	1	**6.7%**
401 vs. 503	1	33.3%
402 vs. 502	0.438	**2.9%**
402 vs. 503	0.143	26.7%
502 vs. 503	0.429	100.0%

c. Canopy (>2.0 m)
Global R: 0.056, $P = 25.9\%$

Groups	R	P
401 vs. 402	0.5	6.7%
401 vs. 502	0	100.0%
401 vs. 503	1	33.3%
402 vs. 502	-0.047	65.7%
402 vs. 503	-0.179	65.7%
502 vs. 503	-0.179	73.3%

Bolded values are statistically significant at our selected P value threshold.

not differ from any other stratum ($P \geq 20\%$; Table 3-1a, b, c), perhaps reflecting the influence of the small sample size to date (n=2).

The extent of the enormous dissimilarity between field and subcanopy vegetation by stratum is illustrated by MDS (Figure 3-1a, b). In particular, plots 401_V01 and 401_V02 (both of the low-elevation, fine-soil plots), and plot 402_V04 (a low-elevation, coarse-soil site), stand in stark contrast to the subcanopy- and field-layer

a) Field (<0.5 m)

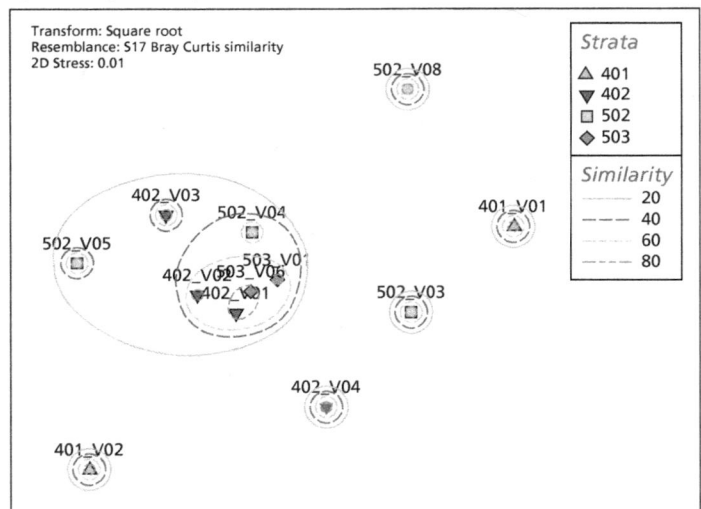

b) Subcanopy (0.5–2.0 m)

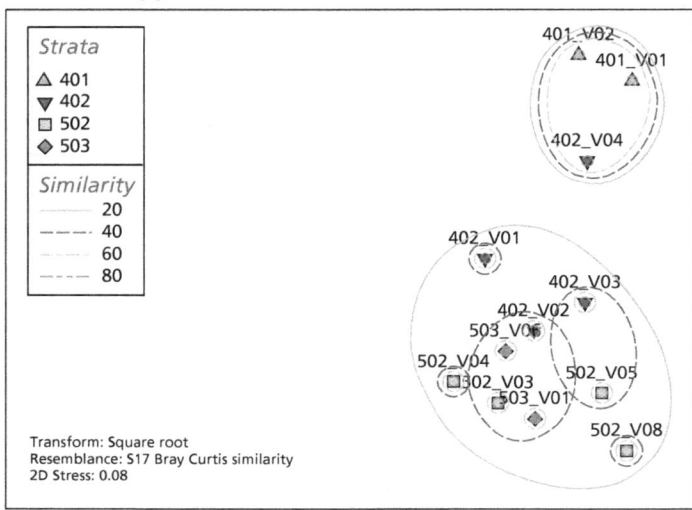

c) Canopy (>2.0 m)

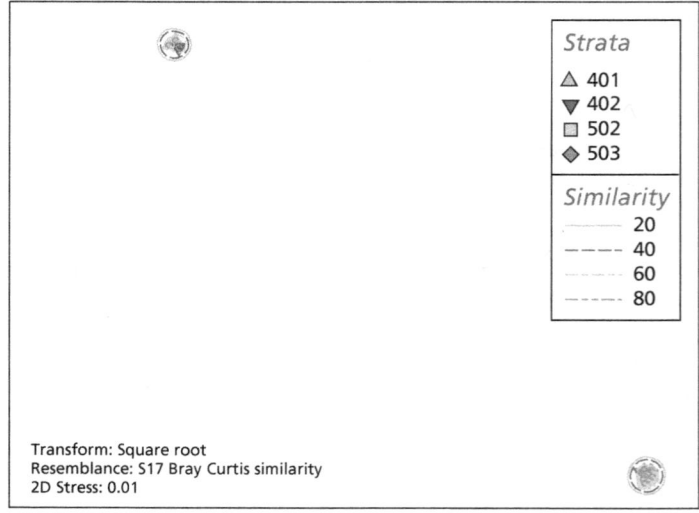

Figure 3-1. Non-metric multidimensional scaling indicating similarity of (a) field, (b) subcanopy, and (c) canopy layer communities, Coronado NMEM, 2009–2010. The distance between any two points increases as their species composition differs.

vegetation of all other plots (Figure 3-1a, b). Canopy vegetation composition was more site-specific for these three plots than for others, as well (Figure 3-1c). For field and subcanopy vegetation, this sharp break in similarity is explained by the tremendous influence of *Eragrostis lehmanniana* on the dissimilarity between plant communities at Coronado NMEM, as illustrated in bubble-plot overlays (in MDS) of the relative abundance of *E. lehmanniana* (Figure 3-2a, b).

A subsequent MDS analysis on the field-layer vegetation of the large cluster of other plots (Figure 3-3) indicates reasonably high similarity across plots, with no obvious patterns by strata.

3.3 Plant species detectability

Line-point intercepts on the 12 monitoring sites sampled in 2009 and 2010 detected 85 perennial species, and employing the frequency subplots added 40 perennial species. However, slope decreased markedly on species accumulation curves (Figure 3-4), suggesting diminishing returns for detecting new species with increased sampling intensity.

3.4 Power to detect trends

3.4.1 Plant lifeforms and common perennial species

Our proposed sampling design generally met or exceeded our expectations for statistical power to detect trends in common perennial species based on our design criteria (i.e., to detect a 10% absolute change in foliar cover with 90% power and 10% chance of a false change error). The exceptions were:

1. *Eragrostis lehmanniana* in the field layer of non-rocky (401) and rocky (402) plots below 6,000' (Appendix A, Table A1), in which we estimate that we can detect an 18% and 12% change (respectively) in foliar cover, reducing the parkwide change detection to 11%—just missing our change criteria (Table A1). Taller *E. lehmanniana* were also somewhat problematic in the subcanopy of rocky sites below 6,000' (402), with an estimated detection of 11% (Table A2).

2. Emory oak (*Quercus emoryi*) in the canopy of rocky sites below 6,000' (402), with an estimated detected change of 11% (Table A3).

Plot-specific detail is provided in Appendix B, Tables B1–B3.

3.4.2 Uncommon perennial species

Our design met or exceeded our sampling objectives for detecting trends for many uncommon perennial species (i.e., to detect at least a 10% change in within-plot frequency with 90% power and 10% chance of false change error) for species encountered only in frequency subplots. Forty-seven species with relatively high within-plot frequencies and high variance had less power to detect change (Table A4) based on frequency. However, all but four of these species (wild dwarf morning-glory, *Evolvulus arizonicus*; dwarf false pennyroyal, *Hedeoma nana*; firecrackerbush, *Bouvardia ternifolia*; and walkingstick cactus, *Cylindropuntia spinosior*) were also detected as vegetation cover along the line-point transects, which provide far more precise estimates and improved statistical power than frequency (Appendix A, Tables A1–3). Plot-level results are given in Appendix B, Table B4.

3.4.3 Soil parameters

Our design met or exceeded our sampling objectives (i.e., to detect at least a 10% change in cover with 90% power and 10% chance of false change error) for nearly all soil substrate types at the proposed sampling intensity (Table A5). The only exception was gravel cover on bedrock/rock outcrop sites above 6,000' (503 stratum), for which we estimated a change detection of 14%.

Power for detecting change in the surface soil aggregate stability index (i.e., to detect at least a 10% change in stability index value with 90% power and 10% chance of false change error) was similarly good, with only stability under vegetation cover on loamy sites below 6,000' (401 stratum) just exceeding (by 0.1%) our criteria. As we are seeing in other parks, the alternate measure of stability, the percentage of samples which are "very stable" (index value = 6) has very poor power to detect change (Table A5).

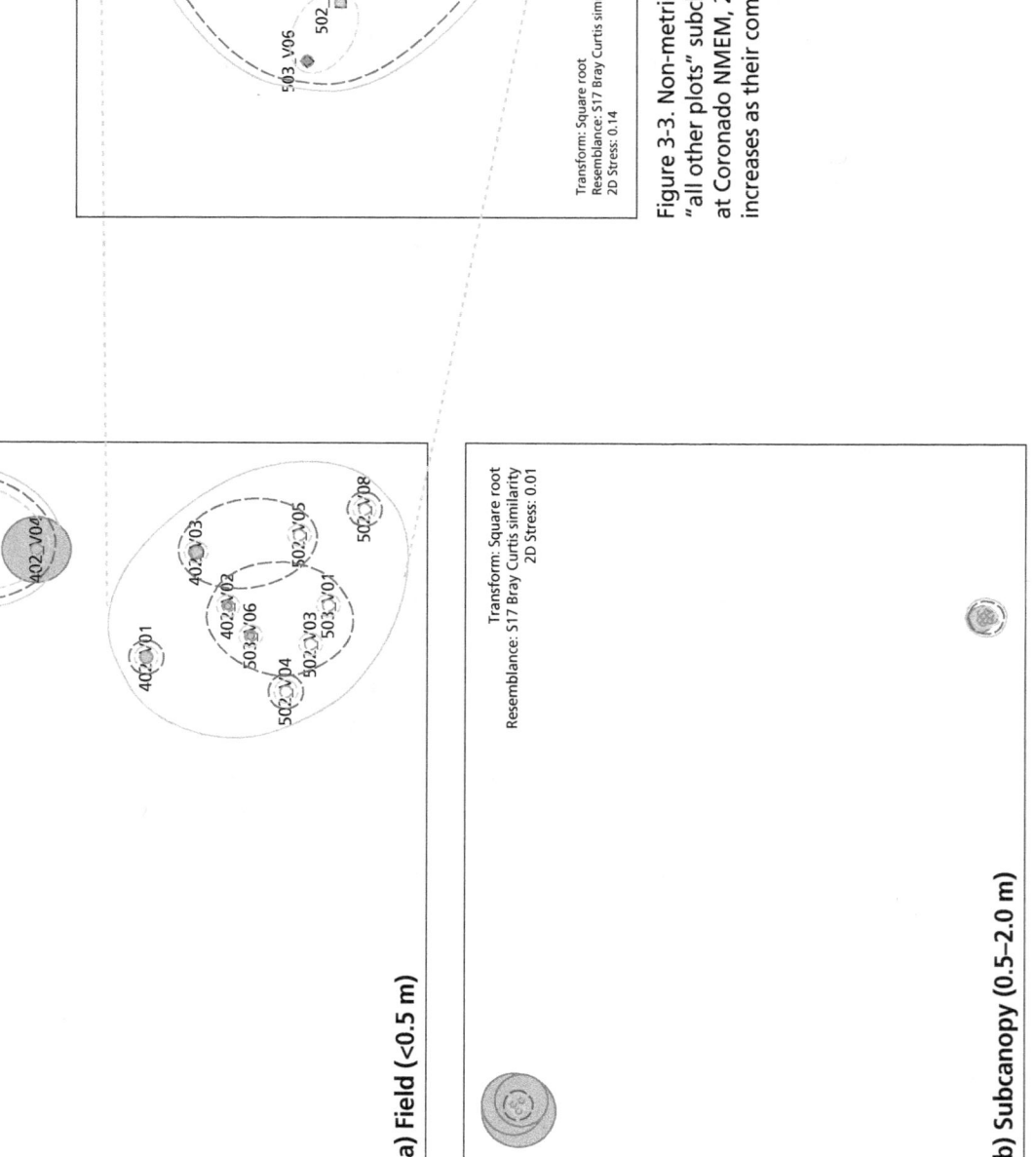

a) Field (<0.5 m)

Transform: Square root
Resemblance: S17 Bray Curtis similarity
2D Stress: 0.08

Transform: Square root
Resemblance: S17 Bray Curtis similarity
2D Stress: 0.14

Figure 3-3. Non-metric multidimensional scaling indicates similarity of "all other plots" subcluster (from Figure 3-2a) for field layer-vegetation at Coronado NMEM, 2009–2010. The distance between any two points increases as their composition and structure differ.

b) Subcanopy (0.5–2.0 m)

Transform: Square root
Resemblance: S17 Bray Curtis similarity
2D Stress: 0.01

Figure 3-2. Bubble-plot overlay of *Eragrostis lehmanniana* cover on MDS for (a) field and (b) subcanopy indicates the massive influence of this exotic grass on plant communities at Coronado NMEM (2009–2010 data). The size of the bubbles indicates the relative cover of this noxious species. The distance between any two points increases as their composition and structure differ.

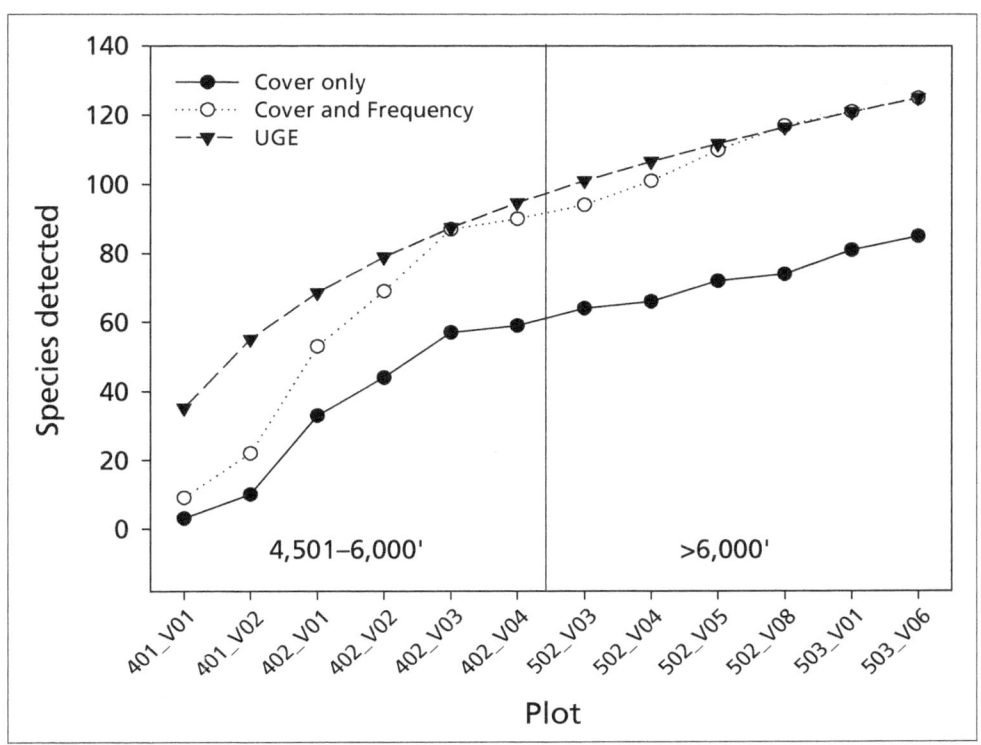

Figure 3-4. Species area curves for cover and frequency data collected on terrestrial vegetation and soils plots at Coronado NMEM, 2009–2010. Curves show cumulative numbers of species detected as plots are added. UGE = mean species accumulation curve with samples entered in random order (Ugland et al. 2003).

4 Discussion

4.1 Are the strata effective?

Our results suggest that vegetation communities are well-differentiated by elevation (below vs. above 6,000'), one of our two stratification variables. However, the influence of soil rock fragments is more difficult to assess, in large part because of the erratic cover of Lehmann lovegrass (*Eragrostis lehmanniana*), an important non-native invasive grass.

On both low-elevation sites without rocky soils (401 stratum), *E. lehmanniana* cover was dominant, with some of the highest cover values for an individual species that the network has ever recorded for a SODN park. This is in keeping with the conventional wisdom of park and network staff: the greater water holding capacity of fine soils retains winter rains for longer periods of time, favoring *E. lehmanniana*—a warm season grass that breaks dormancy much earlier than native bunchgrasses—such that it comes to dominate these sites.

However, one of the four rocky sites (402), plot 4, also had superabundant *E. lehmanniana* cover, with very little cover of native bunchgrasses and other species. This contradicts the parallel conventional wisdom for *E. lehmanniana* encroachment into semi-desert grasslands, which is that the relatively dry soil conditions of rocky sites favors native grassland and savanna species, and restricts *E. lehmanniana* to be a relatively minor component of the community.

Because we collected soil samples at each long-term monitoring plot, we were able to verify that plot 4 is correctly classified as "very to extremely rocky" (with 50% surface rock fragments), suggesting that the conventional wisdom for *E. lehmanniana* distribution does not hold, at least for this particular site at Coronado NMEM. This may have consequences for the soil element of our stratification approach, due to the profound influence that *E. lehmanniana* abundance has on overall grassland communities.

Our inconclusive results regarding the efficacy of stratification by soil type were further complicated by the small number of plots (2 each) that have been sampled to date, particularly in the low-elevation sites with few rock fragments (401), and high-elevation bedrock sites (503). To better assess the value of our design, we propose an adjusted sampling schedule (Table 4-1) that accelerates sampling of plots in the 401 and 503 strata, adds an additional 503 plot, and will allow us to reassess this issue in our 2011 data summary using a more complete dataset. If warranted by the 2011 data, we may combine some strata.

4.2 Does the sample size meet our criteria?

Estimated statistical power to detect change was generally good based on the proposed sample size. We nearly always met (and often exceeded) our target criteria for change detection for perennial species. However, there were a few important exceptions.

As described in Section 4.1, *E. lehmanniana* was found in an almost three-phase distribution: superabundance in the low-elevation non-rocky soils (and one low-elevation rocky site), minor cover (<10%) on most low-elevation rocky sites, and near absence on sites above 6,000' (but see plot 503_V06, Table B1b). This tremendous site-to-site variability resulted in poor estimated power to detect trends in *E. lehmanniana* (and consequently, perennial grass lifeforms and total plant cover), particularly on low-elevation sites. We conclude that power to detect trends in *E. lehmanniana* is not adequate, given the central

Table 4-1. Adjusted sampling schedule for Coronado National Memorial.

Strata	Plots sampled		Plots not yet sampled		
	2009	2010	2011	2012	2013
401 (non-rocky soils, 4,501–6,000')	1	2	3, 4		
402 (rocky soils, 4,501–6,000')	1, 2	3, 4	5, 6, 7	8, 9, 10	11, 12, 13
502 (rocky soils, >6,000')	3, 4	5, 8	9, 10	11, 12	13, 14
503 (bedrock or rock outcrops, >6,000')	1	6	8, 9		

Values are the site labels within each stratum. Plots in bold red have not been sampled to date. Section 2.2.2 describes the stratification scheme. Table 2-3 shows the original sampling schedule.

importance of this problematic species to park management.

The other power issues also involved the low-elevation strata. The common tree, emory oak (*Quercus emoryi*) dominated many sites in the 402 (low-elevation, rocky soils) stratum, but was subdominant in others, and absent on the plot (402_V04; see Table B1a) that contained high *E. lehmanniana* cover. As a result, power for trend detection slightly (by 3%) missed our criteria. Standing dead perennial plants ("snags") were similarly inconsistent across low-elevation sites with few rocks (401 stratum).

Resolving the soil type–stratum grouping issue (see Section 4.1) should reduce within-stratum variability and will be our first approach to improving trend detection. However, after incorporating the 2011 data and strata evaluation into our analyses, it may be necessary to add additional plots to meet our objectives. We will reassess this issue in the 2011 data summary.

We detected only 125 (19%) of the 649 known plant species for Coronado NMEM in this monitoring (Schmidt et al. 2007). However, less than one-third of the sites have been sampled; the sampling frame excludes aquatic, riparian, and xeroripiarian sites that are biodiversity hotspots; and this protocol does not call for identification of annuals to species. In addition, the flattening line of the species accumulation curve suggested that our species detectability was quite reasonable. As a result, we do not recommend any increases in sample size for species detectability at this time. We will reassess this conclusion annually in future data summaries.

4.3 Implications for terrestrial vegetation and soils monitoring

This effort entailed some of the first terrestrial vegetation and soils monitoring in the SODN. Therefore, much of our focus was on evaluating the efficacy of the sampling and response designs to support improvement of the protocol. We found the plot sampling design to be efficient: most plots were sampled within 2–4 hours, including tasks that will not need to be repeated in successive visits (e.g., initial plot layout, permanent marking and mapping, and collection of in situ soil and landscape parameters). All sites are relatively accessible for day trips, although border security remains a fluctuating issue relative to safe access at the park.

After comparing these results with our monitoring objectives, we conclude that the sampling design is appropriate, based on our criteria. We will adjust our sampling program in 2011 to better evaluate the value of stratification, so as to permit further adjustments as needed before the completion of the five-year sampling period in 2013.

5 Literature Cited

Bailey, R. G. 1998. Ecoregions: The ecosystem geography of the oceans and continents. New York: Springer-Verlag Inc.

Bennetts, R. E., J. E. Gross, K. Cahill, C. L. McIntyre, B. B. Bingham, J. A. Hubbard, L. Cameron, and S. L. Carter. 2007. Linking monitoring to management and planning: Assessments points as a generalized approach. The George Wright Forum 24(2):59–77.

Bingham, B. B., R. E. Bennetts, and J. A. Hubbard. 2007. Integrating science and management: the road to Rico-Chico. The George Wright Forum 24(2):21–25.

Bonham, C. D. 1989. Measurements for terrestrial vegetation. New York: Wiley-Interscience.

Clarke, K. R., and R. M. Warwick. 2001. Change in marine communities: An approach to statistical analysis and interpretation, 2nd edition. PRIMER-E, Plymouth, U.K.

Elzinga, C. L., D. W. Salzer, and J. W. Willoughby. 1998. Measuring and monitoring plant populations. Bureau of Land Management, Denver, Colorado. BLM Technical Reference 1730-1.

Herrick, J. E., J. W. Van Zee, K. M. Havstad, L. M. Burkett, and W. G. Whitford. 2005a. Monitoring manual for grassland, shrubland and savanna ecosystems. Volume 1: Quick start. USDA-ARS Jornada Experimental Range, Las Cruces, New Mexico.

——. 2005b. Monitoring manual for grassland, shrubland, and savanna ecosystems. Volume II: Design, supplementary methods, and interpretation. Tucson: University of Arizona Press.

Hubbard, J. A., C. L. McIntyre, S. E. Studd, T. W. Nauman, D. Angell, M. K. Connor, and K. Beaupré. In review. Terrestrial vegetation and soils monitoring protocol and standard operating procedures for the Sonoran and Chihuahuan Desert Networks.

Hubbard, J. A., S. Studd, and C. McIntyre. 2010. Terrestrial vegetation and soils monitoring at Fort Bowie National Historic Site: 2008 status report. Natural Resource Technical Report NPS/SODN/NRTR—2010/368. National Park Service, Fort Collins, Colorado.

McAuliffe, J. R. 1999. The Sonoran Desert: Landscape complexity and ecological diversity. Pages 68–114 in R. H. Robichaux, ed., Ecology of Sonoran Desert plants and plant communities. Tucson: University of Arizona Press.

National Park Service. 2005. Sonoran Desert Network monitoring plan. National Park Service, Sonoran Desert Network, Tucson, Arizona.

Schmidt, C.A., B. F. Powell, D. E. Swann, and W.L. Halvorson. 2007. Vascular plant and vertebrate inventory of Coronado National Memorial. USGS OFR 2007-1393. USGS Southwest Biological Science Center, Sonoran Desert Research Station, University of Arizona, Tucson, Arizona.

Shreve, F. 1951. Vegetation of the Sonoran Desert. Washington, D.C.: Carnegie Institution of Washington Publication no. 591.

Stehman, S. V. 1999. Basic probabilistic sampling for thematic mapper accuracy assessment. International Journal of Remote Sensing 20:2347–2366.

Stevens, D. L., and A. R. Olsen. 2004. Spatially balanced sampling of natural resources. Journal of the American Statistical Association 99:262–278.

Theobald, D. M., D. L. Stevens, Jr., D. White, N. S. Urquart, A. R. Olsen, and J. B. Norman. 2007. Using GIS to generate spatially balanced designs for natural resource applications. Environmental Management 40:134–146.

Ugland, K. I., J. S. Gray, and K. E. Ellingsen. 2003. The species-accumulation curve and estimation of species richness. Journal of Animal Ecology 72:888–897.

Whittaker, R. H. 1975. Communities and ecosystems. Indianapolis, In.: MacMillan.

Appendix A. Supplementary Data Tables by Stratum

These data represent only 40% of the proposed sample size, and are presented to evaluate power to detect change only - ecological conclusions data should NOT be drawn from this data!

Unless otherwise noted, the following categories and notations apply throughout this appendix:

Stratum	Elevation	Description	Number of plots
401	4,501–6,000'	Non-rocky	2 (of 4)
402	4,501–6,000'	Very to Extremely Rocky	4 (of 13)
502	>6,000'	Very to Extremely Rocky	4 (of 10)
503	>6,000'	Bedrock or Rock Outcrop	2 (of 3)
Parkwide			12 (of 30)

Layer	Stature
Field	<0.5 m
Subcanopy	0.5–2.0 m
Canopy	>2.0 m

- AVG = average
- MDC = minimum detectable change (% cover)
- n = required number of plots for power criteria
- SD = standard deviation
- Sdiff = standard deviation of the differences
- SE = standard error

- Highlighted species failed to meet our statistical power criteria.
- Bolded species are non-native.

Table A1. Cover values (%) for species measured in the field layer of terrestrial vegetation and soils plots by stratum, Coronado NMEM, 2009–2010.

Species	401				402				502				503				Parkwide (12 of 30)			
	AVG	SE	MDC	n=	AVG	SE	MDC	n=	AVG	SE	MDC	n=	AVG	SE	MDC	n=	AVG	SE	MDC	n=
Forb/Herb																				
Ambrosia	---	---	5%	0	---	---	5%	0	---	---	5%	0	1.0%	1.0%	5%	1	0.2%	0.17%	5%	1
Artemisia ludoviciana	---	---	5%	0	1.0%	1.0%	5%	1	1.1%	1.0%	5%	1	1.3%	0.8%	5%	1	0.9%	0.47%	5%	1
Bommeria hispida	---	---	5%	0	---	---	5%	0	---	---	5%	0	0.2%	0.2%	5%	1	0.0%	0.03%	5%	1
Cheilanthes	---	---	5%	0	0.1%	0.1%	5%	1	0.1%	0.1%	5%	1	0.4%	0.4%	5%	1	0.1%	0.08%	5%	1
Conyza canadensis	0.2%	0.2%	5%	1	0.2%	0.2%	5%	1	---	---	5%	0	0.2%	0.2%	5%	1	0.1%	0.08%	5%	1
Dalea	---	---	5%	0	0.7%	0.7%	5%	1	---	---	5%	0	---	---	5%	0	0.2%	0.24%	5%	1
Gnaphalium	---	---	5%	0	---	---	5%	0	0.2%	0.2%	5%	1	---	---	5%	0	0.1%	0.07%	5%	1
Hedeoma dentata	---	---	5%	0	---	---	5%	0	---	---	5%	0	0.2%	0.2%	5%	1	0.0%	0.03%	5%	1
Hedeoma nana	---	---	5%	0	---	---	5%	0	0.2%	0.1%	5%	1	---	---	5%	0	0.1%	0.05%	5%	1
Ipomoea	---	---	5%	0	0.1%	0.1%	5%	1	0.1%	0.1%	5%	1	---	---	5%	0	0.1%	0.05%	5%	1
Lasianthaea podocephala	---	---	5%	0	0.3%	0.3%	5%	1	---	---	5%	0	---	---	5%	0	0.1%	0.10%	5%	1
Pseudognaphalium canescens	---	---	5%	0	0.1%	0.1%	5%	1	---	---	5%	0	---	---	5%	0	0.0%	0.03%	5%	1
Stachys coccinea	---	---	5%	0	---	---	5%	0	---	---	5%	0	0.2%	0.2%	5%	1	0.0%	0.03%	5%	1
Graminoid																				
Aristida sp.	---	---	5%	0	0.3%	0.2%	5%	1	---	---	5%	0	---	---	5%	0	0.1%	0.07%	5%	1
Aristida purpurea	---	---	5%	0	0.1%	0.1%	5%	1	0.2%	0.1%	5%	1	---	---	5%	0	0.1%	0.05%	5%	1
Aristida schiedeana	---	---	5%	0	4.9%	2.5%	5%	5	4.1%	1.8%	5%	3	7.1%	1.7%	5%	1	4.2%	1.15%	5%	3
Aristida ternipes	0.2%	0.2%	5%	1	5.0%	2.1%	5%	4	1.6%	1.0%	5%	1	1.9%	1.9%	5%	2	2.5%	0.93%	5%	2
Bothriochloa barbinodis	---	---	5%	0	1.8%	1.2%	5%	2	2.0%	0.7%	5%	1	---	---	5%	0	1.3%	0.51%	5%	1
Bouteloua curtipendula	---	---	5%	0	8.5%	2.4%	5%	4	17.7%	6.7%	9%	10	4.2%	0.8%	5%	1	9.4%	2.92%	5%	18
Bouteloua gracilis	0.2%	0.2%	5%	1	0.5%	0.4%	5%	1	0.1%	0.1%	5%	1	---	---	5%	0	0.2%	0.14%	5%	1
Bouteloua hirsuta	0.2%	0.2%	5%	1	---	---	5%	0	1.3%	0.7%	5%	1	1.5%	1.5%	5%	1	0.7%	0.33%	5%	1
Bouteloua repens	---	---	5%	0	---	---	5%	0	0.3%	0.3%	5%	1	---	---	5%	0	0.1%	0.10%	5%	1
Bromus sp.	---	---	5%	0	---	---	5%	0	0.1%	0.1%	5%	1	---	---	5%	0	0.0%	0.03%	5%	1
Digitaria californica	---	---	5%	0	1.1%	0.6%	5%	1	---	---	5%	0	0.2%	0.2%	5%	1	0.4%	0.25%	5%	1
Elionurus barbiculmis	---	---	5%	0	0.5%	0.3%	5%	1	0.7%	0.6%	5%	1	4.8%	0.2%	5%	1	1.2%	0.53%	5%	1
Eragrostis intermedia	---	---	5%	0	5.5%	2.8%	5%	6	3.9%	1.6%	5%	2	2.7%	1.0%	5%	1	3.6%	1.14%	5%	3

Table A1. Cover values (%) for species measured in the field layer of terrestrial vegetation and soils plots by stratum, Coronado NMEM, 2009–2010, cont.

Species	401				402				502				503				Parkwide (12 of 30)			
	AVG	SE	MDC	n=	AVG	SE	MDC	n=	AVG	SE	MDC	n=	AVG	SE	MDC	n=	AVG	SE	MDC	n=
Graminoid, cont.																				
Eragrostis lehmanniana	70.4%	11.3%	18%	4	13.0%	9.8%	12%	12	---	---	5%	0	5.0%	5.0%	9%	3	16.9%	8.10%	11%	28
Heteropogon contortus	---	---	5%	0	0.8%	0.8%	5%	1	---	---	5%	0	0.6%	0.6%	5%	1	0.4%	0.29%	5%	1
Leptochloa dubia	---	---	5%	0	2.8%	1.0%	5%	1	2.0%	1.1%	5%	1	---	---	5%	0	1.6%	0.57%	5%	1
Lycurus phleoides	---	---	5%	0	---	---	5%	0	0.7%	0.7%	5%	1	---	---	5%	0	0.2%	0.24%	5%	1
Lycurus setosus	---	---	5%	0	---	---	5%	0	1.3%	0.3%	5%	1	1.0%	1.0%	5%	1	0.6%	0.24%	5%	1
Muhlenbergia emersleyi	---	---	5%	0	0.7%	0.5%	5%	1	10.7%	4.2%	6%	9	9.0%	5.6%	10%	3	5.3%	2.05%	5%	9
Schizachyrium sp.	---	---	5%	0	1.4%	1.1%	5%	1	3.0%	2.8%	5%	6	4.4%	2.3%	5%	2	2.2%	1.03%	5%	3
Schizachyrium cirratum	---	---	5%	0	2.2%	2.2%	5%	4	---	---	5%	0	1.9%	1.9%	5%	2	1.0%	0.77%	5%	2
Sporobolus wrightii	---	---	5%	0	0.6%	0.6%	5%	1	---	---	5%	0	---	---	5%	0	0.2%	0.21%	5%	1
Trachypogon spicatus	---	---	5%	0	---	---	5%	0	---	---	5%	0	3.3%	3.3%	5%	4	0.6%	0.56%	5%	1
Subshrub																				
Acacia angustissima	---	---	5%	0	0.9%	0.9%	5%	1	0.8%	0.5%	5%	1	0.2%	0.2%	5%	1	0.6%	0.34%	5%	1
Baccharis bigelovii	---	---	5%	0	0.2%	0.2%	5%	1	---	---	5%	0	---	---	5%	0	0.1%	0.07%	5%	1
Brickellia sp.	---	---	5%	0	0.5%	0.2%	5%	1	1.1%	0.7%	5%	1	0.8%	0.8%	5%	1	0.7%	0.26%	5%	1
Brickellia californica	---	---	5%	0	1.4%	1.4%	5%	2	1.8%	1.8%	5%	3	0.6%	0.6%	5%	1	1.1%	0.70%	5%	2
Brickellia venosa	---	---	5%	0	0.1%	0.1%	5%	1	0.5%	0.5%	5%	1	---	---	5%	0	0.2%	0.17%	5%	1
Desmodium cinerascens	---	---	5%	0	---	---	5%	0	---	---	5%	0	1.0%	1.0%	5%	1	0.2%	0.17%	5%	1
Ericameria laricifolia	---	---	5%	0	---	---	5%	0	---	---	5%	0	1.5%	1.5%	5%	1	0.2%	0.24%	5%	1
Eriogonum wrightii	0.8%	0.8%	5%	1	---	---	5%	0	---	---	5%	0	---	---	5%	0	0.1%	0.14%	5%	1
Galium wrightii	---	---	5%	0	---	---	5%	0	---	---	5%	0	1.0%	1.0%	5%	1	0.2%	0.17%	5%	1
Gymnosperma glutinosum	---	---	5%	0	0.2%	0.2%	5%	1	0.3%	0.3%	5%	1	---	---	5%	0	0.2%	0.12%	5%	1
Nolina microcarpa	---	---	5%	0	1.3%	1.3%	5%	2	0.5%	0.5%	5%	1	---	---	5%	0	0.6%	0.44%	5%	1
Solanum elaeagnifolium	---	---	5%	0	0.1%	0.1%	5%	1	---	---	5%	0	---	---	5%	0	0.0%	0.03%	5%	1
Trichostema arizonicum	---	---	5%	0	1.3%	1.1%	5%	1	0.1%	0.1%	5%	1	1.5%	0.6%	5%	1	0.7%	0.40%	5%	1

Table A1. Cover values (%) for species measured in the field layer of terrestrial vegetation and soils plots by stratum, Coronado NMEM, 2009–2010, cont.

Species	401				402				502				503				Parkwide (12 of 30)			
	AVG	SE	MDC	n=	AVG	SE	MDC	n=	AVG	SE	MDC	n=	AVG	SE	MDC	n=	AVG	SE	MDC	n=
Shrub																				
Aloysia wrightii	---	---	5%	0	---	---	5%	0	0.2%	0.2%	5%	1	---	---	5%	0	0.1%	0.07%	5%	1
Arctostaphylos pungens	---	---	5%	0	0.1%	0.1%	5%	1	---	---	5%	0	---	---	5%	0	0.0%	0.03%	5%	1
Baccharis pteronioides	---	---	5%	0	0.1%	0.1%	5%	1	---	---	5%	0	0.2%	0.2%	5%	1	0.1%	0.05%	5%	1
Calliandra eriophylla	---	---	5%	0	0.1%	0.1%	5%	1	---	---	5%	0	---	---	5%	0	0.0%	0.03%	5%	1
Calliandra humilis	0.2%	0.2%	5%	1	0.2%	0.2%	5%	1	---	---	5%	0	---	---	5%	0	0.1%	0.07%	5%	1
Cercocarpus montanus	---	---	5%	0	---	---	5%	0	0.4%	0.3%	5%	1	---	---	5%	0	0.1%	0.11%	5%	1
Garrya wrightii	---	---	5%	0	---	---	5%	0	0.4%	0.4%	5%	1	---	---	5%	0	0.1%	0.14%	5%	1
Mimosa aculeaticarpa	---	---	5%	0	0.2%	0.2%	5%	1	0.2%	0.2%	5%	1	---	---	5%	0	0.1%	0.09%	5%	1
Rhus trilobata	---	---	5%	0	---	---	5%	0	0.4%	0.4%	5%	1	---	---	5%	0	0.1%	0.14%	5%	1
Rhus virens	---	---	5%	0	0.2%	0.2%	5%	1	0.6%	0.6%	5%	1	---	---	5%	0	0.3%	0.21%	5%	1
Succulent																				
Agave palmeri	---	---	5%	0	---	---	5%	0	---	---	5%	0	0.2%	0.2%	5%	1	0.0%	0.03%	5%	1
Agave parryi	---	---	5%	0	0.1%	0.1%	5%	1	---	---	5%	0	---	---	5%	0	0.0%	0.03%	5%	1
Dasylirion wheeleri	---	---	5%	0	1.0%	0.9%	5%	1	2.6%	0.3%	5%	1	2.5%	0.0%	5%	1	1.6%	0.42%	5%	1
Echinocereus pectinatus	---	---	5%	0	---	---	5%	0	---	---	5%	0	0.2%	0.2%	5%	1	0.0%	0.03%	5%	1
Yucca madrensis	---	---	5%	0	0.1%	0.1%	5%	1	0.4%	0.2%	5%	1	0.8%	0.0%	5%	0	0.3%	0.12%	5%	1
Tree																				
Juniperus deppeana	---	---	5%	0	---	---	5%	0	0.1%	0.1%	5%	1	---	---	5%	0	0.0%	0.03%	5%	1
Pinus discolor	---	---	5%	0	---	---	5%	0	0.9%	0.9%	5%	1	0.2%	0.2%	5%	1	0.3%	0.31%	5%	1
Prosopis velutina	0.8%	0.8%	5%	1	---	---	5%	0	---	---	5%	0	---	---	5%	0	0.1%	0.14%	5%	1
Quercus arizonica	---	---	5%	0	0.7%	0.7%	5%	1	---	---	5%	0	---	---	5%	0	0.2%	0.24%	5%	1
Quercus emoryi	---	---	5%	0	1.8%	1.5%	5%	2	1.5%	1.2%	5%	1	1.5%	1.5%	5%	1	1.3%	0.63%	5%	1
Vine																				
Ipomoea coccinea	---	---	5%	0	0.4%	0.4%	5%	1	0.4%	0.4%	5%	1	---	---	5%	0	0.3%	0.19%	5%	1
Ipomoea longifolia	---	---	5%	0	---	---	5%	0	0.4%	0.4%	5%	1	---	---	5%	0	0.1%	0.14%	5%	1
Phaseolus	---	---	5%	0	2.5%	2.5%	5%	5	---	---	5%	0	---	---	5%	0	0.8%	0.83%	5%	2

Table A1. Cover values (%) for species measured in the field layer of terrestrial vegetation and soils plots by stratum, Coronado NMEM, 2009–2010, cont.

Species	401				402				502				503				Parkwide (12 of 30)			
	AVG	SE	MDC	n=	AVG	SE	MDC	n=	AVG	SE	MDC	n=	AVG	SE	MDC	n=	AVG	SE	MDC	n=
Lifeform																				
Annual Forb	---	---	5%	0	2.4%	0.9%	5%	1	0.9%	0.3%	5%	1	1.5%	1.5%	5%	1	1.4%	0.42%	5%	1
Annual Grass	---	---	5%	0	0.3%	0.3%	5%	1	1.6%	1.1%	5%	1	---	---	5%	0	0.6%	0.40%	5%	1
Perennial Forb	0.2%	0.2%	5%	1	2.6%	2.2%	5%	4	1.8%	1.0%	5%	1	3.5%	1.5%	5%	1	2.1%	0.81%	5%	2
Perennial Grass	71.0%	11.0%	17%	4	49.9%	3.1%	5%	7	49.6%	4.1%	6%	9	47.5%	5.0%	9%	3	52.9%	3.27%	5%	22
Subshrub	0.8%	0.8%	5%	1	5.9%	2.5%	5%	5	5.2%	1.3%	5%	2	6.7%	2.5%	5%	3	5.0%	1.07%	5%	3
Shrub	0.2%	0.2%	5%	1	0.9%	0.3%	5%	1	2.3%	1.6%	5%	2	0.2%	0.2%	5%	1	1.1%	0.56%	5%	1
Succulent	---	---	5%	0	1.3%	0.9%	5%	1	3.0%	0.4%	5%	1	3.8%	0.4%	5%	1	2.0%	0.49%	5%	1
Tree	0.8%	0.8%	5%	1	2.5%	1.5%	5%	2	2.5%	2.2%	5%	4	1.7%	1.3%	5%	1	2.1%	0.85%	5%	2
Snag	20.6%	12.7%	19%	4	14.8%	8.0%	10%	11	7.2%	2.4%	5%	4	9.4%	1.0%	5%	1	12.3%	3.31%	5%	23
Vine	---	---	5%	0	2.9%	2.9%	5%	6	0.8%	0.8%	5%	1	---	---	5%	0	1.3%	0.99%	5%	2
Total	73.1%	9.0%	14%	4	68.8%	6.1%	8%	10	67.7%	3.5%	5%	9	64.8%	0.6%	5%	1	68.5%	2.50%	5%	13

Table A2. Cover values (%) for species measured in the subcanopy layer of terrestrial vegetation and soils plots, Coronado NMEM, 2009–2010.

Species	401				402				502				503				Parkwide			
	AVG	SE	MDC	n=	AVG	SE	MDC	n=	AVG	SE	MDC	n=	AVG	SE	MDC	n=	AVG	SE	MDC	n=
Forb/Herb																				
Ambrosia sp.	---	---	5%	0	---	---	5%	0	---	---	5%	0	0.2%	0.2%	5%	1	0.0%	0.03%	5%	1
Artemisia ludoviciana	---	---	5%	0	---	---	5%	0	0.1%	0.1%	5%	1	---	---	5%	0	0.0%	0.03%	5%	1
Conyza sp.	---	---	5%	0	0.1%	0.1%	5%	1	---	---	5%	0	---	---	5%	0	0.0%	0.03%	5%	1
Dalea sp.	---	---	5%	0	0.1%	0.1%	5%	1	---	---	5%	0	---	---	5%	0	0.0%	0.03%	5%	1
Graminoid																				
Aristida schiedeana	---	---	5%	0	0.6%	0.4%	5%	1	1.5%	0.9%	5%	1	1.0%	0.2%	5%	1	0.9%	0.33%	5%	1
Aristida ternipes	0.8%	0.8%	5%	1	2.0%	1.0%	5%	1	0.1%	0.1%	5%	1	0.2%	0.2%	5%	1	0.9%	0.41%	5%	1
Bothriochloa barbinodis	---	---	5%	0	1.5%	1.2%	5%	1	0.1%	0.1%	5%	1	---	---	5%	0	0.5%	0.41%	5%	1
Bouteloua curtipendula	---	---	5%	0	1.8%	0.7%	5%	1	1.9%	0.7%	5%	1	0.8%	0.4%	5%	1	1.4%	0.37%	5%	1
Bouteloua gracilis	---	---	5%	0	0.2%	0.2%	5%	1	---	---	5%	0	---	---	5%	0	0.1%	0.07%	5%	1
Bouteloua hirsuta	---	---	5%	0	0.2%	0.2%	5%	1	---	---	5%	0	---	---	5%	0	0.1%	0.07%	5%	1
Elionurus barbiculmis	---	---	5%	0	0.0%	0.0%	5%	0	0.2%	0.2%	5%	1	1.7%	0.0%	5%	1	0.3%	0.19%	5%	1
Eragrostis intermedia	---	---	5%	0	1.8%	0.9%	5%	1	0.5%	0.3%	5%	1	0.2%	0.2%	5%	1	0.8%	0.37%	5%	1
Eragrostis lehmanniana	**33.3%**	**3.3%**	**5%**	**4**	**10.0%**	**8.9%**	**11%**	**12**	---	---	**5%**	**0**	**0.2%**	**0.2%**	**5%**	**1**	**8.9%**	**4.47%**	**6%**	**29**
Heteropogon contortus	---	---	5%	0	---	---	5%	0	---	---	5%	0	0.2%	0.2%	5%	1	0.0%	0.03%	5%	1
Leptochloa dubia	---	---	5%	0	2.1%	1.0%	5%	1	0.5%	0.3%	5%	1	0.2%	0.2%	5%	1	0.9%	0.41%	5%	1
Muhlenbergia emersleyi	---	---	5%	0	---	---	5%	0	3.2%	1.8%	5%	3	2.5%	2.1%	5%	2	1.5%	0.74%	5%	2
Schizachyrium sp.	---	---	5%	0	0.3%	0.3%	5%	1	1.1%	0.7%	5%	1	1.5%	1.5%	5%	1	0.7%	0.34%	5%	1
Schizachyrium cirratum	---	---	5%	0	0.3%	0.3%	5%	1	---	---	5%	0	0.2%	0.2%	5%	1	0.1%	0.11%	5%	1
Sporobolus wrightii	---	---	5%	0	0.3%	0.3%	5%	1	---	---	5%	0	---	---	5%	0	0.1%	0.10%	5%	1
Subshrub																				
Acacia angustissima	---	---	5%	0	0.1%	0.1%	5%	1	---	---	5%	0	---	---	5%	0	0.0%	0.03%	5%	1
Brickellia sp.	---	---	5%	0	0.3%	0.3%	5%	1	0.3%	0.3%	5%	1	0.6%	0.6%	5%	1	0.3%	0.16%	5%	1
Brickellia californica	---	---	5%	0	1.5%	1.5%	5%	2	1.6%	1.6%	5%	2	---	---	5%	0	1.0%	0.68%	5%	1
Desmodium cinerascens	---	---	5%	0	---	---	5%	0	---	---	5%	0	0.8%	0.8%	5%	1	0.1%	0.14%	5%	1
Ericameria laricifolia	---	---	5%	0	0.1%	0.1%	5%	1	---	---	5%	0	0.4%	0.4%	5%	1	0.1%	0.07%	5%	1

Table A2. Cover values (%) for species measured in the subcanopy layer of terrestrial vegetation and soils plots, Coronado NMEM, 2009–2010, cont.

Species	401				402				502				503				Parkwide			
	AVG	SE	MDC	n=	AVG	SE	MDC	n=	AVG	SE	MDC	n=	AVG	SE	MDC	n=	AVG	SE	MDC	n=
Subshrub, cont.																				
Gymnosperma glutinosum	---	---	5%	0	0.2%	0.2%	5%	1	---	---	5%	0	---	---	5%	0	0.1%	0.07%	5%	1
Nolina microcarpa	---	---	5%	0	0.8%	0.8%	5%	1	0.4%	0.3%	5%	1	---	---	5%	0	0.4%	0.29%	5%	1
Trichostema arizonicum	---	---	5%	0	0.1%	0.1%	5%	1	---	---	5%	0	---	---	5%	0	0.0%	0.03%	5%	1
Shrub																				
Aloysia wrightii	---	---	5%	0	---	---	5%	0	0.1%	0.1%	5%	1	---	---	5%	0	0.0%	0.03%	5%	1
Arctostaphylos pungens	---	---	5%	0	0.2%	0.2%	5%	1	---	---	5%	0	---	---	5%	0	0.1%	0.07%	5%	1
Baccharis pteronioides	---	---	5%	0	---		5%	0	0.1%	0.1%	5%	1	---	---	5%	0	0.0%	0.03%	5%	1
Cercocarpus montanus	---	---	5%	0	---	---	5%	0	2.7%	1.6%	5%	2	---	---	5%	0	0.9%	0.62%	5%	1
Garrya wrightii	---	---	5%	0	---	---	5%	0	1.5%	1.5%	5%	2	---	---	5%	0	0.5%	0.49%	5%	1
Mimosa aculeaticarpa	---	---	5%	0	---	---	5%	0	0.4%	0.3%	5%	1	---	---	5%	0	0.1%	0.11%	5%	1
Rhus trilobata	---	---	5%	0	---	---	5%	0	0.5%	0.5%	5%	1	---	---	5%	0	0.2%	0.17%	5%	1
Rhus virens	---	---	5%	0	---	---	5%	0	0.9%	0.9%	5%	1	---	---	5%	0	0.3%	0.31%	5%	1
Succulent																				
Dasylirion wheeleri	---	---	5%	0	0.2%	0.2%	5%	1	1.9%	0.8%	5%	1	1.5%	0.6%	5%	1	0.9%	0.36%	5%	1
Yucca madrensis	---	---	5%	0	0.1%	0.1%	5%	1	0.6%	0.4%	5%	1	0.8%	0.4%	5%	1	0.4%	0.16%	5%	1
Tree																				
Juniperus deppeana	---	---	5%	0	---	---	5%	0	0.8%	0.6%	5%	1	---	---	5%	0	0.3%	0.21%	5%	1
Pinus discolor	---	---	5%	0	---	---	5%	0	2.0%	2.0%	5%	3	1.3%	1.3%	5%	1	0.9%	0.67%	5%	1
Prosopis velutina	0.8%	0.8%	5%	1	0.6%	0.6%	5%	1	---	---	5%	0	---	---	5%	0	0.3%	0.24%	5%	1
Quercus arizonica	---	---	5%	0	5.0%	4.5%	6%	10	0.2%	0.2%	5%	1	---	---	5%	0	1.7%	1.52%	5%	5
Quercus emoryi	---	---	5%	0	13.1%	7.1%	9%	11	3.1%	1.8%	5%	3	12.9%	6.7%	12%	3	7.6%	2.89%	5%	18
Phaseolus sp.	---	---	5%	0	0.2%	0.2%	5%	1	0.0%	0.0%	5%	0	---	---	5%	0	0.1%	0.07%	5%	1

Table A2. Cover values (%) for species measured in the subcanopy layer of terrestrial vegetation and soils plots, Coronado NMEM, 2009–2010, cont.

Species	401				402				502				503				Parkwide			
	AVG	SE	MDC	n=	AVG	SE	MDC	n=	AVG	SE	MDC	n=	AVG	SE	MDC	n=	AVG	SE	MDC	n=
Lifeform																				
Annual Forb	---	---	5%	0	0.2%	0.1%	5%	1	0.1%	0.1%	5%	1	---	---	5%	0	0.1%	0.05%	5%	1
Annual Grass	---	---	5%	0	---	---	5%	0	---	---	5%	0	---	---	5%	0	0.0%	0.00%	5%	0
Perennial Forb	---	---	5%	0	0.2%	0.1%	5%	1	0.1%	0.1%	5%	1	0.2%	0.2%	5%	1	0.1%	0.06%	5%	1
Perennial Grass	34.2%	2.5%	5%	3	21.0%	6.8%	8%	13	9.2%	2.4%	5%	4	8.8%	1.3%	5%	1	17.2%	3.56%	5%	26
Subshrub	---	---	5%	0	3.1%	2.3%	5%	4	2.3%	1.4%	5%	2	1.9%	0.2%	5%	1	2.1%	0.88%	5%	2
Shrub	---	---	5%	0	0.2%	0.2%	5%	1	6.3%	4.4%	6%	10	---	---	5%	0	2.2%	1.60%	5%	6
Succulent	---	---	5%	0	0.3%	0.2%	5%	1	2.5%	0.7%	5%	1	2.3%	1.0%	5%	1	1.3%	0.42%	5%	1
Tree	0.8%	0.8%	5%	1	18.8%	5.9%	7%	13	6.1%	3.8%	6%	7	14.2%	5.4%	10%	3	10.8%	3.04%	5%	19
Snag	0.2%	0.2%	5%	1	1.3%	0.4%	5%	1	0.5%	0.1%	5%	1	0.4%	0.4%	5%	1	0.7%	0.18%	5%	1
Vine	---	---	5%	0	0.2%	0.2%	5%	1	---	---	5%	0	---	---	5%	0	0.1%	0.07%	5%	1
Total	35.0%	1.7%	5%	1	44.1%	2.9%	5%	6	26.6%	5.8%	8%	9	27.3%	2.7%	5%	3	33.9%	3.07%	5%	20

Table A3. Cover values (%) for species measured in the canopy layer of terrestrial vegetation and soils plots, Coronado NMEM, 2009–2010.

Species	401				402				502				503				Parkwide			
	AVG	SE	MDC	n=	AVG	SE	MDC	n=	AVG	SE	MDC	n=	AVG	SE	MDC	n=	AVG	SE	MDC	n=
Forb/Herb																				
Echevaria bartramii	---	---	5%	0	---	---	5%	0	0.1%	0.1%	5%	1	---	---	5%	0	0.0%	0.03%	5%	1
Najas marina	---	---	5%	0	---	---	5%	0	0.1%	0.1%	5%	1	---	---	5%	0	0.0%	0.03%	5%	1
Shrub																				
Cercocarpus montanus	---	---	5%	0	---	---	5%	0	0.5%	0.5%	5%	1	---	---	5%	0	0.2%	0.17%	5%	1
Tree																				
Juniperus deppeana	---	---	5%	0	---	---	5%	0	0.9%	0.9%	5%	1	---	---	5%	0	0.3%	0.31%	5%	1
Pinus discolor	---	---	5%	0	---	---	5%	0	0.7%	0.7%	5%	1	0.4%	0.4%	5%	1	0.3%	0.25%	5%	1
Prosopis velutina	---	---	5%	0	0.6%	0.6%	5%	1	---	---	5%	0	---	---	5%	0	0.2%	0.21%	5%	1
Quercus arizonica	---	---	5%	0	5.9%	5.1%	6%	13	0.8%	0.8%	5%	1	---	---	5%	0	2.3%	1.76%	5%	7
Quercus emoryi	---	---	5%	0	18.0%	10.1%	12%	13	0.9%	0.9%	5%	1	13.3%	2.9%	5%	3	8.5%	3.93%	5%	32
Lifeform																				
Annual Forb	---	---	5%	0	---	---	5%	0	---	---	5%	0	---	---	5%	0	0.0%	0.00%	5%	0
Annual Grass	---	---	5%	0	---	---	5%	0	---	---	5%	0	---	---	5%	0	0.0%	0.00%	5%	0
Perennial Forb	---	---	5%	0	---	---	5%	0	0.2%	0.2%	5%	1	---	---	5%	0	0.1%	0.07%	5%	1
Perennial Grass	---	---	5%	0	---	---	5%	0	---	---	5%	0	---	---	5%	0	0.0%	0.00%	5%	0
Subshrub	---	---	5%	0	---	---	5%	0	---	---	5%	0	---	---	5%	0	0.0%	0.00%	5%	0
Shrub	---	---	5%	0	---	---	5%	0	0.5%	0.5%	5%	1	---	---	5%	0	0.2%	0.17%	5%	1
Succulent	---	---	5%	0	---	---	5%	0	---	---	5%	0	---	---	5%	0	0.0%	0.00%	5%	0
Tree	---	---	5%	0	24.6%	8.7%	10%	13	3.4%	1.4%	5%	2	13.8%	2.5%	5%	3	11.6%	4.05%	6%	24
Snag	---	---	5%	0	0.1%	0.1%	5%	1	---	---	5%	0	---	---	5%	0	0.0%	0.03%	5%	1
Vine	---	---	5%	0	---	---	5%	0	---	---	5%	0	---	---	5%	0	0.0%	0.00%	5%	0
Total	---	---	5%	0	24.6%	8.7%	10%	13	4.2%	0.9%	5%	1	13.8%	2.5%	5%	3	11.9%	3.99%	6%	23

Table A4. Within-plot and landscape frequency (%) for all species sampled on monitoring plots, Coronado NMEM, 2009–2010.

Scientific name	401 Within-plot Mean	SE	Stratum	402 Within-plot Mean	SE	Stratum	502 Within-plot Mean	SE	Stratum	503 Within-plot Mean	SE	Stratum	All strata Within-plot Mean	SE	Landscape	MDC	n
Forb/Herb																	
Ambrosia sp.	--	--	--	--	--	--	--	--	--	30%	30.0%	33%	5%	5%	8%	7%	27
Artemisia ludoviciana	50%	50.0%	50%	35%	23.6%	50%	55%	17.1%	100%	80%	20.0%	67%	52%	12%	75%	16%	29
Bommeria hispida	--	--	--	35%	17.1%	75%	10%	10.0%	25%	30%	10.0%	67%	20%	7%	50%	10%	28
Castilleja tenuiflora	--	--	--	--	--	--	5%	5.0%	25%	--	--	--	2%	2%	8%	5%	6
Chamaesyce sp.	--	--	--	5%	5.0%	25%	--	--	--	--	--	--	2%	2%	8%	5%	6
Cheilanthes sp.	--	--	--	15%	9.6%	50%	20%	8.2%	75%	80%	20.0%	67%	25%	9%	58%	12%	29
Commelina erecta	--	--	--	--	--	--	5%	5.0%	25%	--	--	--	2%	2%	8%	5%	6
Conyza sp.	10%	10.0%	--	35%	17.1%	75%	--	--	--	10%	10.0%	33%	13%	7%	33%	10%	26
Conyza canadensis	--	--	50%	20%	20.0%	25%	10%	10.0%	25%	--	--	--	12%	7%	25%	10%	27
Dalea sp.	--	--	--	25%	25.0%	25%	10%	10.0%	25%	10%	10.0%	33%	13%	9%	25%	12%	27
Evolvulus arizonicus	--	--	--	25%	25.0%	25%	--	--	--	--	--	--	8%	8%	8%	11%	30
Gnaphalium sp.	50%	50.0%	50%	--	--	--	15%	15.0%	25%	10%	10.0%	33%	15%	9%	25%	13%	26
Hedeoma dentata	--	--	--	35%	23.6%	50%	5%	5.0%	25%	40%	40.0%	33%	20%	10%	33%	13%	32
Hedeoma nana	--	--	--	--	--	--	30%	23.8%	50%	50%	50.0%	33%	18%	11%	25%	15%	29
Ipomoea sp.	--	--	--	30%	19.1%	50%	15%	15.0%	25%	10%	10.0%	33%	17%	8%	33%	11%	28
Lasianthaea podocephala	--	--	--	25%	25.0%	25%	--	--	--	--	--	--	8%	8%	8%	11%	30
Machaeranthera tagetina	--	--	--	20%	20.0%	25%	--	--	--	--	--	--	7%	7%	8%	9%	29
Mirabilis longiflora	--	--	--	--	--	--	5%	5.0%	25%	--	--	--	2%	2%	8%	5%	6
ANNUAL FORB	--	--	--	65%	12.6%	100%	40%	8.2%	100%	30%	30.0%	33%	40%	9%	75%	12%	28
Najas marina	--	--	--	--	--	--	5%	5.0%	25%	--	--	--	2%	2%	8%	5%	6
Oenothera sp.	--	--	--	5%	5.0%	25%	15%	15.0%	25%	--	--	--	5%	5%	8%	7%	27
Pellaea sp.	--	--	--	--	--	--	--	--	--	10%	10.0%	33%	3%	2%	17%	5%	11
Pellaea truncata	--	--	--	5%	5.0%	25%	5%	5.0%	25%	--	--	--	2%	2%	8%	5%	6
Porophyllum ruderale	--	--	--	--	--	--	10%	10.0%	25%	--	--	--	3%	3%	8%	5%	23
Pseudognaphalium canescens	--	--	--	5%	5.0%	25%	10%	10.0%	25%	--	--	--	5%	4%	17%	5%	27
Sida abutifolia	20%	20.0%	50%	--	--	--	**10%**	**10.0%**	**25%**	20%	20.0%	33%	**7%**	**4%**	**17%**	**6%**	**29**
Stachys coccinea	--	--	--	--	--	--	5%	5.0%	25%	--	20.0%	33%	5%	4%	17%	5%	27
Aristida sp.	--	--	--	15%	9.6%	50%	--	--	--	--	--	--	5%	4%	17%	5%	27

Table A4. Within-plot and landscape frequency (%) for all species sampled on monitoring plots, Coronado NMEM, 2009–2010, cont.

Scientific name	401 Within-plot Mean	401 Within-plot SE	401 Stratum	402 Within-plot Mean	402 Within-plot SE	402 Stratum	502 Within-plot Mean	502 Within-plot SE	502 Stratum	503 Within-plot Mean	503 Within-plot SE	503 Stratum	All strata Within-plot Mean	All strata Within-plot SE	All strata Landscape	MDC	n
Graminoid																	
Aristida purpurea	--	--	--	--	--	--	10%	5.8%	50%	--	--	--	3%	2%	17%	5%	11
Aristida schiedeana	--	--	--	55%	20.6%	75%	65%	20.6%	100%	100%	0.0%	67%	57%	13%	75%	17%	28
Aristida ternipes	50%	50.0%	50%	70%	17.3%	100%	40%	18.3%	75%	50%	30.0%	67%	53%	11%	83%	15%	29
Bothriochloa barbinodis	--	--	--	85%	9.6%	100%	70%	12.9%	100%	20%	0.0%	67%	55%	11%	83%	15%	28
Bouteloua curtipendula	--	--	--	95%	5.0%	100%	90%	10.0%	100%	100%	0.0%	67%	78%	11%	83%	15%	29
Bouteloua gracilis	50%	50.0%	50%	35%	22.2%	75%	5%	5.0%	25%	--	--	--	22%	11%	42%	15%	27
Bouteloua hirsuta	30%	10.0%	100%	20%	14.1%	50%	35%	22.2%	75%	70%	30.0%	67%	35%	10%	75%	14%	28
Bouteloua repens	--	--	--	10%	5.8%	50%	35%	20.6%	50%	--	--	--	15%	8%	33%	11%	26
Bromus sp.	--	--	--	5%	5.0%	25%	10%	10.0%	25%	--	--	--	5%	4%	17%	5%	27
Digitaria californica	20%	20.0%	50%	35%	5.0%	100%	15%	15.0%	25%	--	--	--	20%	7%	50%	9%	27
Echinochloa sp.	--	--	--	--	--	--	5%	5.0%	25%	10%	10.0%	33%	3%	2%	17%	5%	11
Elionurus barbiculmis	--	--	--	25%	12.6%	75%	15%	15.0%	25%	90%	10.0%	67%	28%	11%	50%	14%	30
Eragrostis intermedia	20%	0.0%	100%	85%	9.6%	100%	90%	5.8%	100%	100%	0.0%	67%	78%	9%	100%	12%	27
Eragrostis lehmanniana	**100%**	**0.0%**	**100%**	**85%**	**15.0%**	**100%**	**5%**	**5.0%**	**25%**	**70%**	**30.0%**	**67%**	**58%**	**13%**	**75%**	**18%**	**28**
Heteropogon contortus	--	--	--	25%	15.0%	50%	--	--	--	30%	10.0%	67%	13%	6%	33%	9%	25
Leptochloa dubia	10%	10.0%	50%	60%	18.3%	100%	65%	17.1%	100%	20%	0.0%	67%	47%	10%	92%	14%	28
Lycurus sp.	--	--	--	20%	20.0%	25%	--	--	--	--	--	--	7%	7%	8%	9%	29
Lycurus phleoides	--	--	--	--	--	--	10%	10.0%	25%	--	--	--	3%	3%	8%	5%	23
Lycurus setosus	10%	10.0%	50%	15%	9.6%	50%	95%	5.0%	100%	30%	30.0%	33%	43%	12%	67%	17%	27
Muhlenbergia emersleyi	--	--	--	50%	20.8%	75%	100%	0.0%	100%	100%	0.0%	67%	67%	13%	75%	17%	30
Muhlenbergia polycaulis	--	--	--	--	--	--	5%	5.0%	25%	--	--	--	2%	2%	8%	5%	6
Muhlenbergia tenuifolia	--	--	--	--	--	--	5%	5.0%	25%	--	--	--	2%	2%	8%	5%	6
ANNUAL GRASS	--	--	--	5%	5.0%	25%	15%	15.0%	25%	80%	20.0%	67%	7%	5%	17%	7%	28
Schizachyrium sp.	--	--	--	45%	22.2%	75%	40%	24.5%	50%	40%	20.0%	67%	42%	12%	58%	17%	28
Schizachyrium cirratum	--	--	--	20%	20.0%	25%	--	--	--	20%	20.0%	33%	10%	7%	17%	10%	27

Table A4. *Within-plot and landscape frequency (%) for all species sampled on monitoring plots, Coronado NMEM, 2009–2010, cont.*

| | 401 | | | 402 | | | 502 | | | 503 | | | All strata | | | | |
Scientific name	Within-plot Mean	SE	Stratum	Within-plot Mean	SE	Stratum	Within-plot Mean	SE	Stratum	Within-plot Mean	SE	Stratum	Within-plot Mean	SE	Landscape	MDC	n
Graminoid, cont.																	
Sporobolus wrightii	--	--	--	10%	10.0%	25%	--	--	--	--	--	--	3%	3%	8%	5%	23
Trachypogon spicatus	--	--	--	--	--	--	--	--	--	30%	30.0%	33%	5%	5%	8%	7%	27
Subshrub																	
Acacia angustissima	--	--	--	55%	22.2%	75%	55%	18.9%	75%	60%	40.0%	67%	47%	12%	67%	16%	29
Bouvardia ternifolia	--	--	--	25%	18.9%	50%	35%	17.1%	75%	20%	20.0%	33%	23%	9%	50%	12%	28
Brickellia sp.	--	--	--	45%	20.6%	75%	60%	24.5%	75%	20%	20.0%	33%	38%	12%	58%	16%	29
Brickellia californica	--	--	--	15%	15.0%	25%	25%	25.0%	25%	60%	40.0%	67%	23%	12%	33%	16%	27
Brickellia venosa	--	--	--	5%	5.0%	25%	20%	20.0%	25%	--	--	--	8%	7%	17%	9%	29
Dalea albiflora	--	--	--	--	--	--	--	--	--	10%	10.0%	33%	2%	2%	8%	5%	6
Desmodium cinerascens	--	--	--	--	--	--	--	--	--	40%	40.0%	33%	7%	7%	8%	9%	29
Ericameria laricifolia	--	--	--	15%	15.0%	25%	--	--	--	100%	0.0%	67%	22%	12%	25%	16%	28
Eriogonum wrightii	40%	40.0%	50%	25%	25.0%	25%	5%	5.0%	25%	--	--	--	17%	10%	25%	14%	27
Galium wrightii	--	--	--	10%	10.0%	25%	--	--	--	30%	30.0%	33%	5%	5%	8%	7%	27
Geranium caespitosum	--	--	--	10%	10.0%	25%	--	--	--	--	--	--	3%	3%	8%	5%	23
Gymnosperma glutinosum	--	--	--	25%	25.0%	25%	40%	18.3%	75%	--	--	--	22%	11%	33%	14%	30
Nolina microcarpa	--	--	--	25%	25.0%	25%	40%	18.3%	75%	--	--	--	22%	11%	33%	14%	30
Solanum elaeagnifolium	--	--	--	30%	19.1%	50%	5%	5.0%	25%	--	--	--	12%	7%	25%	10%	27
Trichostema arizonicum	--	--	--	40%	24.5%	50%	25%	18.9%	50%	90%	10.0%	67%	37%	13%	50%	17%	28
Viguiera cordifolia	--	--	--	--	--	--	5%	5.0%	25%	--	--	--	2%	2%	8%	5%	6
Xanthisma spinulosum	--	--	--	15%	15.0%	25%	--	--	--	--	--	--	5%	5%	8%	7%	27
Shrub																	
Aloysia wrightii	--	--	--	--	--	--	10%	10.0%	25%	--	--	--	3%	3%	8%	5%	23
Arctostaphylos pungens	--	--	--	10%	10.0%	25%	--	--	--	--	--	--	3%	3%	8%	5%	23
Baccharis sp.	--	--	--	5%	5.0%	25%	--	--	--	--	--	--	2%	2%	8%	5%	6
Baccharis pteronioides	50%	50.0%	50%	15%	9.6%	50%	25%	12.6%	75%	10%	10.0%	33%	23%	9%	58%	12%	28

Table A4. Within-plot and landscape frequency (%) for all species sampled on monitoring plots, Coronado NMEM, 2009–2010, cont.

Scientific name	401 Within-plot Mean	SE	Stratum	402 Within-plot Mean	SE	Stratum	502 Within-plot Mean	SE	Stratum	503 Within-plot Mean	SE	Stratum	All strata Within-plot Mean	SE	Landscape	MDC	n
Shrub, cont.																	
Baccharis sarothroides	10%	10.0%	50%	--	--	--	--	--	--	--	--	--	2%	2%	8%	5%	6
Calliandra eriophylla	--	--	--	15%	15.0%	25%	--	--	--	--	--	--	5%	5%	8%	7%	27
Calliandra humilis	10%	10.0%	50%	5%	5.0%	25%	--	--	--	--	--	--	3%	2%	17%	5%	11
Cercocarpus montanus	--	--	--	--	--	--	55%	22.2%	75%	--	--	--	18%	10%	25%	14%	28
Garrya wrightii	--	--	--	--	--	--	40%	24.5%	50%	--	--	--	13%	9%	17%	13%	27
Mimosa aculeaticarpa	10%	10.0%	50%	35%	20.6%	50%	10%	5.8%	50%	10%	10.0%	33%	18%	8%	50%	10%	30
SNAG	90%	10.0%	100%	100%	0.0%	100%	90%	5.8%	100%	100%	0.0%	67%	95%	3%	100%	5%	14
Rhus trilobata	--	--	--	--	--	--	5%	5.0%	25%	--	--	--	2%	2%	8%	5%	6
Rhus virens	--	--	--	15%	15.0%	25%	45%	18.9%	100%	10%	10.0%	33%	22%	9%	50%	12%	29
Rhus virens var. choriophylla	--	--	--	5%	5.0%	25%	5%	5.0%	25%	--	--	--	3%	2%	17%	5%	11
Succulent																	
Agave palmeri	--	--	--	--	--	--	15%	5.0%	75%	60%	40.0%	67%	15%	8%	42%	11%	29
Agave parryi	--	--	--	10%	5.8%	50%	5%	5.0%	25%	--	--	--	5%	3%	25%	5%	14
Cylindropuntia acanthocarpa	--	--	--	5%	5.0%	25%	--	--	--	--	--	--	2%	2%	8%	5%	6
Cylindropuntia leptocaulis	--	--	--	5%	5.0%	25%	--	--	--	--	--	--	2%	2%	8%	5%	6
Cylindropuntia spinosior	--	--	--	30%	12.9%	75%	45%	20.6%	75%	20%	0.0%	67%	28%	9%	67%	12%	27
Cylindropuntia versicolor	--	--	--	15%	15.0%	25%	--	--	--	--	--	--	5%	5%	8%	7%	27
Dasylirion wheeleri	--	--	--	50%	28.9%	50%	100%	0.0%	100%	100%	0.0%	67%	67%	14%	67%	19%	29
Echinocereus pectinatus	--	--	--	5%	5.0%	25%	5%	5.0%	25%	40%	20.0%	67%	10%	5%	33%	7%	29
Succulent, cont.																	
Jatropha macrorhiza	--	--	--	10%	5.8%	50%	--	--	--	--	--	--	3%	2%	17%	5%	11
Opuntia sp.	10%	10.0%	50%	--	--	--	--	--	--	10%	10.0%	33%	3%	2%	17%	5%	11
Opuntia engelmannii	--	--	--	20%	11.5%	50%	5%	5.0%	25%	30%	30.0%	33%	13%	6%	33%	9%	25
Yucca madrensis	--	--	--	30%	12.9%	75%	40%	14.1%	100%	50%	10.0%	67%	32%	8%	75%	10%	30

Table A4. Within-plot and landscape frequency (%) for all species sampled on monitoring plots, Coronado NMEM, 2009–2010, cont.

	401			402			502			503			All strata				
	Within-plot		Stratum	Within-plot		Stratum	Within-plot		Stratum	Within-plot		Stratum	Within-plot		Landscape	MDC	n
Scientific name	Mean	SE		Mean	SE		Mean	SE		Mean	SE		Mean	SE			
Tree																	
Juniperus deppeana	–	–	–	–	–	–	30%	17.3%	75%	–	–	–	10%	7%	25%	9%	29
Pinus discolor	–	–	–	10%	10.0%	25%	10%	10.0%	25%	30%	10.0%	67%	12%	5%	33%	7%	29
Prosopis velutina	20%	20.0%	50%	25%	25.0%	25%	–	–	–	–	–	–	12%	9%	17%	12%	27
Quercus arizonica	–	–	–	25%	18.9%	50%	10%	10.0%	25%	10%	10.0%	33%	13%	7%	33%	10%	26
Quercus emoryi	10%	10.0%	50%	65%	23.6%	75%	55%	20.6%	75%	90%	10.0%	67%	57%	12%	75%	16%	29
Quercus oblongifolia	–	–	–	5%	5.0%	25%	–	–	–	–	–	–	2%	2%	8%	5%	6
Vine																	
Ipomoea coccinea	–	–	–	15%	15.0%	25%	25%	18.9%	50%	–	–	–	13%	8%	25%	11%	27
Ipomoea longifolia	–	–	–	–	–	–	20%	20.0%	25%	–	–	–	7%	7%	8%	9%	29
Maurandella antirrhiniflora	–	–	–	15%	15.0%	25%	–	–	–	–	–	–	5%	5%	8%	7%	27
Phaseolus sp.	–	–	–	25%	25.0%	25%	–	–	–	40%	40.0%	33%	15%	10%	17%	14%	28
Vitis arizonica	–	–	–	–	–	–	5%	5.0%	25%	–	–	–	2%	2%	8%	5%	6
Not identified to species																	
Acourtia sp.	–	–	–	–	–	–	10%	10.0%	25%	50%	50.0%	33%	8%	8%	8%	11%	30
Aster sp.	–	–	–	–	–	–	–	–	–	–	–	–	3%	3%	8%	5%	23
Astrolepis sp.	–	–	–	–	–	25%	–	–	–	20%	20.0%	33%	3%	3%	8%	5%	23
Bidens sp.	–	–	–	10%	10.0%	–	–	–	–	–	–	–	3%	3%	8%	5%	23
Brassica sp.	–	–	–	–	–	–	5%	5.0%	25%	–	–	–	2%	2%	8%	5%	6
Chaenactis sp.	–	–	–	–	–	–	5%	5.0%	25%	–	–	–	2%	2%	8%	5%	6
Commelina sp.	–	–	–	–	–	–	15%	9.6%	50%	50%	30.0%	67%	13%	7%	33%	10%	26
Cyperus sp.	–	–	–	35%	23.6%	50%	–	–	–	50%	10.0%	67%	20%	10%	33%	13%	28
Datura sp.	–	–	–	5%	5.0%	25%	–	–	–	–	–	–	2%	2%	8%	5%	6
Erigeron sp.	70%	10.0%	100%	65%	23.6%	75%	–	–	–	40%	0.0%	67%	40%	12%	58%	16%	27
Eriogonum sp.	20%	0.0%	100%	5%	5.0%	25%	5%	5.0%	25%	–	–	–	7%	3%	33%	5%	17
Galium sp.	–	–	–	5%	5.0%	25%	–	–	–	–	–	–	2%	2%	8%	5%	6
Juncus sp.	–	–	–	–	–	–	–	–	–	10%	10.0%	33%	2%	2%	8%	5%	6
Macranthera sp.	–	–	–	15%	15.0%	25%	–	–	–	10%	10.0%	33%	7%	5%	17%	7%	28
Notholaena sp.	–	–	–	25%	25.0%	25%	10%	10.0%	25%	–	–	–	12%	9%	17%	12%	27
Pseudognaphalium sp.	–	–	–	20%	20.0%	25%	–	–	–	–	–	–	7%	7%	8%	9%	29

Table A4. Within-plot and landscape frequency (%) for all species sampled on monitoring plots, Coronado NMEM, 2009–2010, cont.

Scientific name	401			402			502			503			All strata				
	Within-plot		Stratum	Within-plot		Stratum	Within-plot		Stratum	Within-plot		Stratum	Within-plot		Landscape	MDC	n
	Mean	SE		Mean	SE		Mean	SE		Mean	SE		Mean	SE			
Not identified to species, cont.																	
Rhus sp.	--	--	--	5%	5.0%	25%	--	--	--	--	--	--	2%	2%	8%	5%	6
Viguiera sp.	--	--	--	30%	23.8%	50%	95%	5.0%	100%	100%	0.0%	67%	58%	14%	67%	19%	28

Table A5. Soil substrate (% by class) and surface aggregate stability class (mean and SE) and proportion of samples in "very stable" (=6) category, by stratum, Coronado NMEM, 2009–2010.

Parameter	401				402				502				503				Parkwide			
	AVG	SE	MDC	n=	AVG	SE	MDC	n=	AVG	SE	MDC	n=	AVG	SE	MDC	n=	AVG	SE	MDC	n=
Substrate																				
Bare soil (<2 mm), no overhead cover	0.4%	0.0%	5%	0	0.2%	0.2%	5%	1	1.3%	0.2%	5%	1	1.9%	1.5%	5%	1	0.9%	0.28%	5%	1
Bare soil (<2 mm), under vegetation	12.5%	6.7%	10%	4	10.6%	6.3%	8%	11	8.2%	3.7%	5%	10	6.5%	1.5%	5%	1	9.4%	2.43%	5%	13
Light cyanobacteria	0.8%	0.8%	9%	1	0.2%	0.2%	5%	1	--	--	5%	0	--	--	5%	0	0.2%	0.15%	5%	1
Litter and duff (organic matter)	68.8%	2.1%	7%	1	66.5%	6.6%	8%	12	29.4%	5.1%	7%	10	47.1%	5.0%	9%	3	51.3%	5.76%	8%	27
Dark cyanobacteria	1.0%	1.0%	5%	1	0.3%	0.3%	5%	1	--	--	5%	0	--	--	5%	0	0.3%	0.19%	5%	1
Gravel (2–75 mm)	2.7%	2.7%	5%	3	7.0%	4.3%	5%	13	26.3%	6.4%	9%	9	13.3%	7.9%	14%	3	13.8%	3.79%	5%	30
Lichen	--	--	5%	0	--	--	5%	0	--	--	5%	0	--	--	5%	0	--	--	5%	0
Moss	--	--	5%	0	--	--	5%	0	--	--	5%	0	--	--	5%	0	--	--	5%	0
Rock (76–600 mm)	--	--	5%	0	4.7%	2.6%	5%	5	8.8%	3.1%	5%	7	20.4%	5.0%	9%	3	7.9%	2.35%	5%	12
Lichen on rock	--	--	5%	0	0.1%	0.1%	5%	1	2.3%	1.5%	5%	2	0.8%	0.8%	5%	1	0.9%	0.56%	5%	1
Plant base	13.8%	3.7%	6%	4	9.5%	2.1%	5%	4	15.1%	2.2%	5%	4	8.1%	0.6%	5%	1	11.8%	1.36%	5%	4
Bedrock	--	--	5%	0	0.9%	0.8%	5%	1	8.6%	1.0%	5%	1	2.3%	1.9%	5%	2	3.6%	1.19%	5%	3
Surface Soil Aggregate Stability																				
Under cover																				
Average soil stability	4.77	0.69	1.1	4	4.76	0.23	0.3	10	4.79	0.33	0.5	8	3.77	0.08	0.2	2	4.61	0.19	0.3	20
% samples "very stable"	47%	10%	15%	4	53.4%	7.8%	7%	11	46.2%	9.2%	13%	9	33.9%	0.5%	1%	3	46.6%	3.98%	6%	23
Not under cover																				
Average soil stability	1.00	n/a	n/a	n/a	2.75	1.18	1.2	13	3.11	0.64	0.9	9	3.58	0.02	0.1	1	2.89	0.41	0.6	24
% samples "very stable"	0%	n/a	n/a	n/a	0.0%	0.0%	5%	0	10.3%	6.8%	9%	10	26.7%	6.7%	12%	3	9.4%	3.84%	6%	21

Decreasing erosion hazard →

Appendix B. Supplementary Data Tables by Plot

These data represent only 40% of the proposed sample size, and are presented to evaluate power to detect change only - ecological conclusions data should NOT be drawn from this data!

Unless otherwise noted, the following categories and notations apply throughout this appendix:

Stratum	Elevation	Description	Number of plots
401	4,501–6,000'	Non-rocky	2 (of 4)
402	4,501–6,000'	Very to Extremely Rocky	4 (of 13)
502	>6,000'	Very to Extremely Rocky	4 (of 10)
503	>6,000'	Bedrock or Rock Outcrop	2 (of 3)
Parkwide			12 (of 30)

Layer	Stature
Field	<0.5 m
Subcanopy	0.5–2.0 m
Canopy	>2.0 m

- AVG = average
- MDC = minimum detectable change (% cover)
- n = required number of plots for power criteria
- SD = standard deviation
- Sdiff = standard deviation of the differences
- SE = standard error

- Highlighted species failed to meet our statistical power criteria.
- Bolded species are non-native.

Table B1a. Within-plot cover values for species measured in the field layer of terrestrial vegetation and soils plots, low-elevation strata, Coronado NMEM, 2009–2010.

Species	401 2009 401_V01	401 2010 401_V02	401 2011 401_V03	401 401_V04	402 2009 402_V01	402 2009 402_V02	402 2010 402_V03	402 2010 402_V04	402 2011 402_V05	402 2011 402_V06	402 2011 402_V07	402 2012 402_V08	402 2012 402_V09	402 2012 402_V10	402 2013 402_V11	402 2013 402_V12	402 2013 402_V13
Forb/Herb																	
Ambrosia	---	---			---	---	---	---									
Artemisia ludoviciana	---	---			---	---	4.17%	---									
Bommeria hispida	---	---			---	---	---	---									
Cheilanthes	---	---			---	---	0.42%	---									
Conyza canadensis	---	0.42%			---	0.83%	---	---									
Dalea	---	---			---	---	2.92%	---									
Gnaphalium	---	---			---	---	---	---									
Hedeoma dentata	---	---			---	---	---	---									
Hedeoma nana	---	---			---	---	---	---									
Ipomoea	---	---			0.42%	---	---	---									
Lasianthaea podocephala	---	---			---	---	1.25%	---									
Pseudognaphalium canescens	---	---			---	---	0.42%	---									
Stachys coccinea	---	---			---	---	---	---									
Graminoid																	
Aristida sp.	---	---			0.42%	0.83%	---	---									
Aristida purpurea	---	---			---	---	0.42%	---									
Aristida schiedeana	---	---			1.67%	11.25%	6.67%	---									
Aristida ternipes	---	---			10.83%	1.25%	5.42%	2.50%									
Bothriochloa barbinodis	---	---			5.42%	0.42%	0.83%	0.42%									
Bouteloua curtipendula	---	---			12.50%	10.42%	9.58%	1.67%									
Bouteloua gracilis	---	---			---	0.42%	0.00%	1.67%									
Bouteloua hirsuta	0.42%	---			---	---	---	---									
Bouteloua repens	---	---			---	---	---	---									
Bromus sp.	---	---			---	---	---	---									
Digitaria californica	---	---			1.25%	0.42%	2.92%	---									
Elionurus barbiculmis	---	---			---	1.25%	0.83%	---									
Eragrostis intermedia	---	---			5.83%	13.33%	2.50%	0.42%									
Eragrostis lehmanniana	**81.67%**	**59.17%**			**6.67%**	**1.25%**	**2.08%**	**42.08%**									
Heteropogon contortus	---	---			3.33%	---	---	---									
Leptochloa dubia	---	---			4.58%	2.92%	3.75%	---									
Lycurus phleoides	---	---			---	---	---	---									
Lycurus setosus	---	---			---	---	---	---									
Muhlenbergia emersleyi	---	---			0.42%	0.42%	2.08%	---									
Schizachyrium sp.	---	---			0.83%	---	4.58%	---									
Schizachyrium cirratum	---	---			---	8.75%	---	---									
Sporobolus wrightii	---	---			2.50%	---	---	---									
Trachypogon spicatus	---	---			---	---	---	---									

Table B1a. Within-plot cover values for species measured in the field layer of terrestrial vegetation and soils plots, low-elevation strata, Coronado NMEM, 2009–2010, cont.

| | 401 | | | | 402 | | | | | | | | | | | | |
| | 2009 | 2010 | 2011 | | 2009 | | 2010 | | 2011 | | | 2012 | | | 2013 | | |
Species	401_V01	401_V02	401_V03	401_V04	402_V01	402_V02	402_V03	402_V04	402_V05	402_V06	402_V07	402_V08	402_V09	402_V10	402_V11	402_V12	402_V13
Subshrub																	
Acacia angustissima	---	---			3.75%	---	---	---									
Baccharis bigelovii	---	---			0.83%	---	---	---									
Brickellia sp.	---	---			0.83%	0.83%	0.42%	---									
Brickellia californica	---	---			---	---	5.42%	---									
Brickellia venosa	---	---			---	---	0.42%	---									
Desmodium cinerascens	---	---			---	---	---	---									
Ericameria laricifolia	---	---			---	---	---	---									
Eriogonum wrightii	---	1.67%			---	---	---	---									
Galium wrightii	---	---			---	---	---	---									
Gymnosperma glutinosum	---	---			---	---	0.83%	---									
Nolina microcarpa	---	---			---	---	5.00%	---									
Solanum elaeagnifolium	---	---			0.42%	---	---	---									
Trichostema arizonicum	---	---			0.42%	4.58%	---	---									
Shrub																	
Aloysia wrightii	---	---			---	---	---	---									
Arctostaphylos pungens	---	---			---	0.42%	---	---									
Baccharis pteronioides	---	---			0.42%	---	---	---									
Calliandra eriophylla	---	---			0.00%	---	---	0.42%									
Calliandra humilis	---	0.42%			---	---	---	0.83%									
Cercocarpus montanus	---	---			---	---	---	---									
Garrya wrightii	---	---			---	---	---	---									
Mimosa aculeaticarpa	---	---			0.83%	---	---	---									
Rhus trilobata	---	---			---	---	---	---									
Rhus virens	---	---			---	0.83%	---	---									
Succulent																	
Agave palmeri	---	---			---	---	---	---									
Agave parryi	---	---			---	---	---	0.42%									
Dasylirion wheeleri	---	---			---	3.75%	0.42%	---									
Echinocereus pectinatus	---	---			---	---	---	---									
Yucca madrensis	---	---			---	---	0.42%	---									
Tree																	
Juniperus deppeana	---	---			---	---	---	---									
Pinus discolor	---	---			---	---	---	---									
Prosopis velutina	---	1.67%			---	---	---	---									
Quercus arizonica	---	---			---	---	2.92%	---									
Quercus emoryi	---	---			6.25%	0.42%	0.42%	---									
Vine																	
Ipomoea coccinea	---	---			---	---	1.67%	---									
Ipomoea longifolia	---	---			---	---	---	---									
Phaseolus	---	---			---	---	10.00%	---									

Table B1a. *Within-plot cover values for species measured in the field layer of terrestrial vegetation and soils plots, low-elevation strata, Coronado NMEM, 2009–2010, cont.*

Species	401 2009 401_V01	401 2010 401_V02	401 2011 401_V03	401_V04	402 2009 402_V01	402 2009 402_V02	402 2010 402_V03	402 2010 402_V04	402 2011 402_V05	402_V06	402_V07	402 2012 402_V08	402_V09	402_V10	402 2013 402_V11	402_V12	402_V13
Lifeform																	
Annual Forb	---	---			5.00%	1.67%	1.25%	1.67%									
Annual Grass	---	---			---	1.25%	---	---									
Perennial Forb	---	0.42%			0.42%	0.83%	9.17%	---									
Perennial Grass	82.08%	60.00%			56.25%	52.92%	41.67%	48.75%									
Subshrub	---	1.67%			6.25%	5.42%	12.08%	---									
Shrub	---	0.42%			1.25%	1.25%	---	1.25%									
Succulent	---	---			---	3.75%	0.83%	0.42%									
Tree	---	1.67%			6.25%	0.42%	3.33%	0.00%									
Snag	7.92%	33.33%			5.83%	6.67%	7.92%	38.75%									
Vine	---	---			---	---	11.67%	---									
Total	82.08%	64.17%			75.42%	67.50%	80.00%	52.08%									

Table B1b. Within-plot cover values for species measured in the field layer of terrestrial vegetation and soils plots, high-elevation strata, Coronado NMEM, 2009–2010.

Species	502 2009 502_V03	502 2009 502_V04	502 2010 502_V05	502 2010 502_V08	502 2011 502_V09	502 2011 502_V10	502 2012 502_V11	502 2012 202_V12	502 2013 502_V13	502 2013 502_V14	503 2009 503_V01	503 2009 503_V06	503 2011 503_V08	503 2011 503_V09
Forb/Herb														
Ambrosia	---	---	---	---							2.08%	---		
Artemisia ludoviciana	0.42%	---	4.17%	---							2.08%	0.42%		
Bommeria hispida	---	---	---	---							---	0.42%		
Cheilanthes	0.42%	---	---	---							---	0.83%		
Conyza canadensis	---	---	---	---							0.42%	---		
Dalea	---	---	---	---							---	---		
Gnaphalium	0.83%	---	---	---							---	---		
Hedeoma dentata	---	---	---	---							0.42%	---		
Hedeoma nana	---	---	0.42%	0.42%							---	---		
Ipomoea	---	---	---	0.42%							---	---		
Lasianthaea podocephala	---	---	---	---							---	---		
Pseudognaphalium canescens	---	---	---	---							---	---		
Stachys coccinea	---	---	---	---							---	0.42%		
Graminoid														
Aristida sp.	---	---	---	---							---	---		
Aristida purpurea	0.42%	---	---	0.42%							---	---		
Aristida schiedeana	8.75%	1.25%	5.00%	1.25%							5.42%	8.75%		
Aristida ternipes	0.83%	0.83%	4.58%	---							3.75%	---		
Bothriochloa barbinodis	1.25%	3.75%	0.42%	2.50%							---	---		
Bouteloua curtipendula	2.92%	32.50%	25.00%	10.42%							5.00%	3.33%		
Bouteloua gracilis	---	---	0.42%	---							---	---		
Bouteloua hirsuta	2.92%	1.67%	0.42%	---							---	2.92%		
Bouteloua repens	1.25%	---	---	---							---	---		
Bromus sp.	---	---	0.42%	---							---	---		
Digitaria californica	---	---	---	---							0.42%	---		
Elionurus barbiculmis	2.50%	---	0.42%	---							4.58%	5.00%		
Eragrostis intermedia	7.92%	1.67%	5.00%	0.83%							1.67%	3.75%		
Eragrostis lehmanniana	---	---	---	---							---	10.00%		
Heteropogon contortus	---	---	---	---							1.25%	---		
Leptochloa dubia	---	2.92%	4.58%	0.42%							---	---		
Lycurus phleoides	---	2.92%	---	---							---	---		
Lycurus setosus	2.08%	1.25%	1.25%	0.42%							---	2.08%		
Muhlenbergia emersleyi	13.33%	5.42%	2.92%	21.25%							14.58%	3.33%		
Schizachyrium sp.	11.25%	---	0.83%	---							2.08%	6.67%		
Schizachyrium cirratum	---	---	---	---							3.75%	---		
Sporobolus wrightii	---	---	---	---							---	---		
Trachypogon spicatus	---	---	---	---							---	6.67%		

Species	502										503			
	2009		2010		2011		2012		2013		2009		2011	
	502_V03	502_V04	502_V05	502_V08	502_V09	502_V10	502_V11	202_V12	502_V13	502_V14	503_V01	503_V06	503_V08	503_V09
Subshrub														
Acacia angustissima	2.08%	---	1.25%	---							0.42%	---		
Baccharis bigelovii	---	---	---	---							---	---		
Brickellia sp.	---	2.08%	---	2.50%							1.67%	---		
Brickellia californica	---	---	7.08%	---							---	1.25%		
Brickellia venosa	---	2.08%	---	---							---	---		
Desmodium cinerascens	---	---	---	---							---	2.08%		
Ericameria laricifolia	---	---	---	---							2.92%	---		
Eriogonum wrightii	---	---	---	---							---	---		
Galium wrightii	---	---	---	---							2.08%	---		
Gymnosperma glutinosum	---	---	---	1.25%							---	---		
Nolina microcarpa	---	2.08%	---	---							---	---		
Solanum elaeagnifolium	---	---	---	---							---	---		
Trichostema arizonicum	0.42%	---	---	---							2.08%	0.83%		
Shrub														
Aloysia wrightii	---	0.83%	---	---							---	---		
Arctostaphylos pungens	---	---	---	---							---	---		
Baccharis pteronioides	---	---	---	---							---	0.42%		
Calliandra eriophylla	---	---	---	---							---	---		
Calliandra humilis	---	---	---	---							---	---		
Cercocarpus montanus	---	---	0.42%	1.25%							---	---		
Garrya wrightii	---	---	---	1.67%							---	---		
Mimosa aculeaticarpa	---	---	0.83%	---							---	---		
Rhus trilobata	---	---	---	1.67%							---	---		
Rhus virens	---	---	---	2.50%							---	---		
Succulent														
Agave palmeri	---	---	---	---							0.42%	---		
Agave parryi	---	---	---	---							---	---		
Dasylirion wheeleri	2.92%	2.08%	2.08%	3.33%							2.50%	2.50%		
Echinocereus pectinatus	---	---	---	---							0.42%	---		
Yucca madrensis	---	---	0.83%	0.83%							0.83%	0.83%		
Tree														
Juniperus deppeana	0.42%	---	---	---							---	---		
Pinus discolor	3.75%	---	---	---							0.42%	---		
Prosopis velutina	---	---	---	---							---	---		
Quercus arizonica	---	---	---	---							---	---		
Quercus emoryi	5.00%	0.83%	---	---							---	2.92%		
Vine														
Ipomoea coccinea	---	---	1.67%	---							---	---		
Ipomoea longifolia	---	---	1.67%	---							---	---		
Phaseolus	---	---	---	---							---	---		

Table B1b. Within-plot cover values for species measured in the field layer of terrestrial vegetation and soils plots, high-elevation strata, Coronado NMEM, 2009–2010, cont.

Species	502 2009		502 2010		502 2011		502 2012		502 2013		503 2009		503 2011	
	502_V03	502_V04	502_V05	502_V08	502_V09	502_V10	502_V11	202_V12	502_V13	502_V14	503_V01	503_V06	503_V08	503_V09
Lifeform														
Annual Forb	1.67%	0.83%	0.83%	0.42%							2.92%	---		
Annual Grass	---	1.67%	---	4.58%							---	---		
Perennial Forb	1.67%	---	4.58%	0.83%							5.00%	2.08%		
Perennial Grass	55.42%	54.17%	51.25%	37.50%							42.50%	52.50%		
Subshrub	2.50%	6.25%	8.33%	3.75%							9.17%	4.17%		
Shrub	---	0.83%	1.25%	7.08%							---	0.42%		
Succulent	2.92%	2.08%	2.92%	4.17%							4.17%	3.33%		
Tree	9.17%	0.83%	---	---							0.42%	2.92%		
Snag	3.33%	3.33%	8.75%	13.33%							10.42%	8.33%		
Vine	---	---	3.33%	---							---	---		
Total	73.33%	66.67%	72.50%	58.33%							64.17%	65.42%		

Table B2a. Within-plot cover values for species measured in the subcanopy layer of terrestrial vegetation and soils plots, low-elevation strata, Coronado NMEM, 2009–2010.

Species	401 2009 401_V01	401 2010 401_V02	401 2011 401_V03	401 2011 401_V04	402 2009 402_V01	402 2009 402_V02	402 2010 402_V03	402 2010 402_V04	402 2011 402_V05	402 2011 402_V06
Forb/Herb										
Ambrosia sp.	---	---			---	---	---	---		
Artemisia ludoviciana	---	---			---	---	---	---		
Conyza sp.	---	---			---	0.42%	---	---		
Dalea sp.	---	---			---	---	0.42%	---		
Graminoid										
Aristida schiedeana	---	---			---	1.67%	0.83%	---		
Aristida ternipes	---	1.67%			5.00%	0.42%	0.83%	1.67%		
Bothriochloa barbinodis	---	---			5.00%	---	0.83%	---		
Bouteloua curtipendula	---	---			0.42%	3.33%	2.50%	0.83%		
Bouteloua gracilis	---	---			---	---	---	0.83%		
Bouteloua hirsuta	---	---			0.83%	---	---	---		
Elionurus barbiculmis	---	---			---	---	---	---		
Eragrostis intermedia	---	---			0.83%	4.58%	0.83%	0.83%		
Eragrostis lehmanniana	36.67%	30.00%			**1.25%**	**0.42%**	**1.67%**	**36.67%**		
Heteropogon contortus	---	---			---	---	---	---		
Leptochloa dubia	---	---			4.17%	0.83%	3.33%	---		
Muhlenbergia emersleyi	---	---			---	---	---	---		
Schizachyrium sp.	---	---			---	---	1.25%	---		
Schizachyrium cirratum	---	---			---	1.25%	---	---		
Sporobolus wrightii	---	---			1.25%	---	---	---		
Subshrub										
Acacia angustissima	---	---			0.42%	---	---	---		
Brickellia sp.	---	---			---	1.25%	---	---		
Brickellia californica	---	---			---	---	5.83%	---		
Desmodium cinerascens	---	---			---	---	---	---		
Ericameria laricifolia	---	---			---	0.42%	---	---		
Gymnosperma glutinosum	---	---			---	---	0.83%	---		
Nolina microcarpa	---	---			---	---	3.33%	---		
Trichostema arizonicum	---	---			---	0.42%	---	---		
Shrub										
Aloysia wrightii	---	---			---	---	---	---		
Arctostaphylos pungens	---	---			---	0.83%	---	---		
Baccharis pteronioides	---	---			---	---	---	---		
Cercocarpus montanus	---	---			---	---	---	---		
Garrya wrightii	---	---			---	---	---	---		
Mimosa aculeaticarpa	---	---			---	---	---	---		
Rhus trilobata	---	---			---	---	---	---		
Rhus virens	---	---			---	---	---	---		

Table B2a. Within-plot cover values for species measured in the subcanopy layer of terrestrial vegetation and soils plots, low-elevation strata, Coronado NMEM, 2009–2010, cont.

	401				402					
	2009	2010	2011		2009		2010		2011	
Species	401_V01	401_V02	401_V03	401_V04	402_V01	402_V02	402_V03	402_V04	402_V05	402_V06
Succulent										
Dasylirion wheeleri	---	---			---	0.83%	---	---		
Yucca madrensis	---	---			---	---	0.42%	---		
Tree										
Juniperus deppeana	---	---			---	---	---	---		
Pinus discolor	---	---			---	---	---	---		
Prosopis velutina	---	1.67%			---	---	---	2.50%		
Quercus arizonica	---	---			---	1.67%	18.33%	---		
Quercus emoryi	---	---			30.83%	17.92%	3.75%	---		
Vine										
Phaseolus sp.	---	---			---	---	0.83%	---		
Lifeform										
Annual Forb	---	---			---	---	0.4%	0.4%		
Annual Grass	---	---			---	---	---	---		
Perennial Forb	---	---			---	0.4%	0.4%	---		
Perennial Grass	36.7%	31.7%			18.8%	12.5%	12.1%	40.8%		
Subshrub	---	---			0.4%	2.1%	10.0%	---		
Shrub	---	---			---	0.8%	---	---		
Succulent	---	---			---	0.8%	0.4%	---		
Tree	---	1.7%			30.8%	19.6%	22.1%	2.5%		
Snag	0.4%	---			1.7%	2.1%	0.4%	0.8%		
Vine	---	---			---	---	0.8%	---		
Total	36.7%	33.3%			50.0%	36.3%	46.3%	43.8%		

Table B2b. Within-plot cover values for species measured in the subcanopy layer of terrestrial vegetation and soils plots, high-elevation strata, Coronado NMEM, 2009–2010.

Species	502 2009 502_V03	502 2009 502_V04	502 2010 502_V05	502 2010 502_V08	502 2011 502_V09	502 2011 502_V10	502 2012 502_V11	502 2012 202_V12	502 2013 502_V13	502 2013 502_V14	503 2009 503_V01	503 2009 503_V06	503 2011 503_V08	503 2011 503_V09
Forb/Herb														
Ambrosia sp.	---	---	---	---							0.42%	---		
Artemisia ludoviciana	---	---	0.42%	---							---	---		
Conyza sp.	---	---	---	---							---	---		
Dalea sp.	---	---	---	---							---	---		
Graminoid														
Aristida schiedeana	3.33%	---	2.50%	---							0.83%	1.25%		
Aristida ternipes	0.42%	---	---	---							0.42%	---		
Bothriochloa barbinodis	---	---	---	0.42%							---	---		
Bouteloua curtipendula	---	1.67%	3.33%	2.50%							1.25%	0.42%		
Bouteloua gracilis	---	---	---	---							---	---		
Bouteloua hirsuta	---	---	---	---							---	---		
Elionurus barbiculmis	0.83%	---	---	---							1.67%	1.67%		
Eragrostis intermedia	1.25%	---	0.83%	---							0.42%	---		
Eragrostis lehmanniana	---	---	---	---							---	**0.42%**		
Heteropogon contortus	---	---	---	---							0.42%	---		
Leptochloa dubia	---	---	1.25%	0.83%							---	0.42%		
Muhlenbergia emersleyi	2.50%	0.42%	1.67%	8.33%							4.58%	0.42%		
Schizachyrium sp.	2.92%	---	1.67%	---							---	2.92%		
Schizachyrium cirratum	---	---	---	---							0.42%	---		
Sporobolus wrightii	---	---	---	---							---	---		
Subshrub														
Acacia angustissima	---	---	---	---							---	---		
Brickellia sp.	---	---	---	1.25%							1.25%	---		
Brickellia californica	---	---	6.25%	---							---	---		
Desmodium cinerascens	---	---	---	---							---	1.67%		
Ericameria laricifolia	---	---	---	---							0.83%	---		
Gymnosperma glutinosum	---	---	---	---							---	---		
Nolina microcarpa	---	1.25%	---	0.42%							---	---		
Trichostema arizonicum	---	---	---	---							---	---		
Shrub														
Aloysia wrightii	---	0.42%	---	---							---	---		
Arctostaphylos pungens	---	---	---	---							---	---		
Baccharis pteronioides	0.42%	---	---	---							---	---		
Cercocarpus montanus	---	---	4.58%	6.25%							---	---		
Garrya wrightii	---	---	---	5.83%							---	---		
Mimosa aculeaticarpa	---	---	0.42%	1.25%							---	---		
Rhus trilobata	---	---	---	2.08%							---	---		
Rhus virens	---	---	---	3.75%							---	---		

Table B2b. Within-plot cover values for species measured in the subcanopy layer of terrestrial vegetation and soils plots, high-elevation strata, Coronado NMEM, 2009–2010, cont.

	502										503			
	2009		2010		2011	2012	2013				2009		2011	
Species	502_V03	502_V04	502_V05	502_V08	502_V09	502_V10	502_V11	202_V12	502_V13	502_V14	503_V01	503_V06	503_V08	503_V09
Succulent														
Dasylirion wheeleri	4.17%	0.83%	0.83%	1.67%							2.08%	0.83%		
Yucca madrensis	---	---	1.25%	1.25%							1.25%	0.42%		
Tree														
Juniperus deppeana	2.50%	---	---	0.83%							---	---		
Pinus discolor	7.92%	---	---	---							2.50%	---		
Prosopis velutina	---	---	---	---							---	---		
Quercus arizonica	---	---	0.83%	---							---	---		
Quercus emoryi	6.67%	5.83%	---	---							6.25%	19.58%		
Vine														
Phaseolus sp.	---	---	---	---							---	---		
Lifeform														
Annual Forb	---	---	0.4%	---							---	---		
Annual Grass	---	---	---	---							---	---		
Perennial Forb	---	---	0.4%	---							0.4%	---		
Perennial Grass	11.3%	2.1%	11.3%	12.1%							10.0%	7.5%		
Subshrub	---	1.3%	6.3%	1.7%							2.1%	1.7%		
Shrub	0.4%	0.4%	5.0%	19.2%							---	---		
Succulent	4.2%	0.8%	2.1%	2.9%							3.3%	1.3%		
Tree	17.1%	5.8%	0.8%	0.8%							8.8%	19.6%		
Snag	0.4%	0.4%	0.4%	0.8%							---	0.8%		
Vine	---	---	---	---							---	---		
Total	32.9%	10.4%	26.3%	36.7%							24.6%	30.0%		

Table B3a. Within-plot cover values (%) for species measured in the canopy layer of terrestrial vegetation and soils plots, low-elevation strata, Coronado NMEM, 2009–2010.

Species	401 2009 401_V01	401 2010 401_V02	401 2011 401_V03	401 2011 401_V04	402 2009 402_V01	402 2009 402_V02	402 2010 402_V03	402 2010 402_V04	402 2011 402_V05	402 2011 402_V06	402 2011 402_V07	402 2012 402_V08	402 2012 402_V09	402 2012 402_V10	402 2013 402_V11	402 2013 402_V12	402 2013 402_V13
Forb/Herb																	
Echevaria bartramii	---	---			---	---	---	---									
Najas marina	---	---			---	---	---	---									
Shrub																	
Cercocarpus montanus	---	---			---	---	---	---									
Tree																	
Juniperus deppeana	---	---			---	---	---	---									
Pinus discolor	---	---			---	---	---	---									
Prosopis velutina	---	---			---	---	---	2.50%									
Quercus arizonica	---	---			---	2.50%	21.25%	---									
Quercus emoryi	---	---			26.67%	42.50%	2.92%	---									
Lifeform																	
Annual Forb	---	---			---	---	---	---									
Annual Grass	---	---			---	---	---	---									
Perennial Forb	---	---			---	---	---	---									
Perennial Grass	---	---			---	---	---	---									
Subshrub	---	---			---	---	---	---									
Shrub	---	---			---	---	---	---									
Succulent	---	---			---	---	---	---									
Tree	---	---			26.7%	45.0%	24.2%	2.5%									
Snag	---	---			---	---	0.4%	---									
Vine	---	---			---	---	---	---									
Total	---	---			26.7%	45.0%	24.2%	2.5%									

Table B3b. Within-plot cover values (%) for species measured in the canopy layer of terrestrial vegetation and soils plots, high-elevation strata, Coronado NMEM, 2009–2010.

| | 502 | | | | | | | | | | 503 | | | |
| | 2009 | | 2010 | | 2011 | | 2012 | | 2013 | | 2009 | | 2011 | |
Species	502_V03	502_V04	502_V05	502_V08	502_V09	502_V10	502_V11	202_V12	502_V13	502_V14	503_V01	503_V06	503_V08	503_V09
Forb/Herb														
Echevaria bartramii	---	---	0.42%	---							---	---		
Najas marina	---	---	0.42%	---							---	---		
Shrub														
Cercocarpus montanus	---	---	---	2.08%							---	---		
Tree														
Juniperus deppeana	3.75%	---	---	---							---	---		
Pinus discolor	2.92%	---	---	---							0.83%	---		
Prosopis velutina	---	---	---	---							---	---		
Quercus arizonica	---	---	3.33%	---							---	---		
Quercus emoryi	---	3.75%	---	---							10.42%	16.25%		
Lifeform														
Annual Forb	---	---	---	---							---	---		
Annual Grass	---	---	---	---							---	---		
Perennial Forb	---	---	---	---							---	---		
Perennial Grass	---	---	---	---							---	---		
Subshrub	---	---	---	---							---	---		
Shrub	---	---	---	2.1%							---	---		
Succulent	---	---	---	---							---	---		
Tree	6.7%	3.8%	3.3%	---							11.3%	16.3%		
Snag	---	---	---	---							---	---		
Vine	---	---	---	---							---	---		
Total	6.7%	3.8%	4.2%	2.1%							11.3%	16.3%		

Table B4a. Within-plot frequency (0–5) for all plots and species sampled on monitoring plots, low-elevation strata, Coronado NMEM, 2009–2010.

Scientific name	401 2009 401_V01	401 2010 401_V02	401 2011 401_V03	401 2011 401_V04	402 2009 402_V01	402 2010 402_V02	402 2010 402_V03	402 2010 402_V04	402 2011 402_V05	402 2011 402_V06	402 2011 402_V07	402 2012 402_V08	402 2012 402_V09	402 2012 402_V10	402 2013 402_V11	402 2013 402_V12	402 2013 402_V13
Forb/Herb																	
Ambrosia sp.	0	0			0	0	0	0									
Artemisia ludoviciana	0	5			2	0	5	0									
Bommeria hispida	0	0			1	2	4	0									
Castilleja tenuiflora	0	0			0	0	0	0									
Chamaesyce sp.	0	0			1	0	0	0									
Cheilanthes sp.	0	0			0	1	2	0									
Commelina erecta	0	0			0	0	0	0									
Conyza sp.	0	0			2	4	1	0									
Conyza canadensis	0	1			0	0	0	4									
Dalea sp.	0	0			0	0	5	0									
Evolvulus arizonicus	0	0			5	0	0	0									
Gnaphalium sp.	5	0			0	0	0	0									
Hedeoma dentata	0	0			0	2	5	0									
Hedeoma nana	0	0			0	0	0	0									
Ipomoea sp.	0	0			4	2	0	0									
Lasianthaea podocephala	0	0			0	0	5	0									
Machaeranthera tagetina	0	0			0	0	0	4									
Mirabilis longiflora	0	0			0	0	0	0									
ANNUAL FORB	0	0			5	3	3	2									
Najas marina	0	0			0	0	0	0									
Oenothera sp.	0	0			0	0	0	0									
Pellaea sp.	0	0			0	0	1	0									
Pellaea truncata	0	0			0	0	0	0									
Porophyllum ruderale	0	0			0	0	0	0									
Pseudognaphalium canescens	0	0			0	0	1	0									
Sida abutifolia	0	2			0	0	0	0									
Stachys coccinea	0	0			0	0	0	0									
Graminoid																	
Aristida sp.	0	0			1	2	0	0									
Aristida purpurea	0	0			0	0	0	0									
Aristida schiedeana	0	0			3	5	3	0									
Aristida ternipes	0	5			5	1	4	4									
Bothriochloa barbinodis	0	0			5	3	4	5									
Bouteloua curtipendula	0	0			5	5	5	4									
Bouteloua gracilis	0	5			1	1	0	5									
Bouteloua hirsuta	2	1			3	1	0	0									
Bouteloua repens	0	0			1	0	0	1									
Bromus sp.	0	0			0	0	1	0									
Digitaria californica	0	2			2	2	2	1									
Echinochloa sp.	0	0			0	0	0	0									
Elionurus barbiculmis	0	0			1	3	1	0									

Table B4a. Within-plot frequency (0–5) for all plots and species sampled on monitoring plots, low-elevation strata, Coronado NMEM, 2009–2010, cont.

| | 401 | | | | 402 | | | | | | | | | | | | |
| | 2009 | 2010 | 2011 | | 2009 | | 2010 | | 2011 | | | 2012 | | | 2013 | | |
Scientific name	401_V01	401_V02	401_V03	401_V04	402_V01	402_V02	402_V03	402_V04	402_V05	402_V06	402_V07	402_V08	402_V09	402_V10	402_V11	402_V12	402_V13
Graminoid, cont.																	
Eragrostis intermedia	1	1			4	5	5	3									
Eragrostis lehmanniana	5	5			5	5	2	5									
Heteropogon contortus	0	0			3	2	0	0									
Leptochloa dubia	1	0			4	5	2	1									
Lycurus sp.	0	0			4	0	0	0									
Lycurus phleoides	0	0			0	0	0	0									
Lycurus setosus	1	0			0	1	2	0									
Muhlenbergia emersleyi	0	0			2	3	5	0									
Muhlenbergia polycaulis	0	0			0	0	0	0									
Muhlenbergia tenuifolia	0	0			0	0	0	0									
ANNUAL GRASS	0	0			0	1	0	0									
Schizachyrium sp.	0	0			3	1	5	0									
Schizachyrium cirratum	0	0			0	4	0	0									
Sporobolus wrightii	0	0			2	0	0	0									
Trachypogon spicatus	0	0			0	0	0	0									
Subshrub																	
Acacia angustissima	0	0			5	2	4	0									
Bouvardia ternifolia	0	0			0	1	4	0									
Brickellia sp.	0	0			4	4	1	0									
Brickellia californica	0	0			0	0	3	0									
Brickellia venosa	0	0			0	0	1	0									
Dalea albiflora	0	0			0	0	0	0									
Desmodium cinerascens	0	0			0	0	0	0									
Ericameria laricifolia	0	0			0	3	0	0									
Eriogonum wrightii	0	4			0	0	0	5									
Galium wrightii	0	0			0	0	0	0									
Geranium caespitosum	0	0			0	2	0	0									
Gymnosperma glutinosum	0	0			0	0	5	0									
Nolina microcarpa	0	0			0	0	5	0									
Solanum elaeagnifolium	0	0			4	2	0	0									
Trichostema arizonicum	0	0			3	5	0	0									
Viguiera cordifolia	0	0			0	0	0	0									
Xanthisma spinulosum	0	0			3	0	0	0									
Shrub																	
Aloysia wrightii	0	0			0	0	0	0									
Arctostaphylos pungens	0	0			0	2	0	0									
Baccharis sp.	0	0			1	0	0	0									
Baccharis pteronioides	0	5			1	0	0	2									
Baccharis sarothroides	0	1			0	0	0	0									
Calliandra eriophylla	0	0			0	0	0	3									
Calliandra humilis	0	1			0	0	0	1									

Table B4a. Within-plot frequency (0–5) for all plots and species sampled on monitoring plots, low-elevation strata, Coronado NMEM, 2009–2010, cont.

| | 401 | | | | 402 | | | | | | | | | | | | |
| | 2009 | 2010 | 2011 | | 2009 | | 2010 | | 2011 | | | 2012 | | | 2013 | | |
Scientific name	401_V01	401_V02	401_V03	401_V04	402_V01	402_V02	402_V03	402_V04	402_V05	402_V06	402_V07	402_V08	402_V09	402_V10	402_V11	402_V12	402_V13
Shrub, cont																	
Cercocarpus montanus	0	0			0	0	0	0									
Garrya wrightii	0	0			0	0	0	0									
Mimosa aculeaticarpa	0	1			4	3	0	0									
SNAG	4	5			5	5	5	5									
Rhus trilobata	0	0			0	0	0	0									
Rhus virens	0	0			0	3	0	0									
Rhus virens var. choriophylla	0	0			0	0	1	0									
Succulent																	
Agave palmeri	0	0			0	0	0	0									
Agave parryi	0	0			0	0	1	1									
Cylindropuntia acanthocarpa	0	0			1	0	0	0									
Cylindropuntia leptocaulis	0	0			0	1	0	0									
Cylindropuntia spinosior	0	0			3	0	2	1									
Cylindropuntia versicolor	0	0			0	3	0	0									
Dasylirion wheeleri	0	0			0	5	5	0									
Echinocereus pectinatus	0	0			1	0	0	0									
Jatropha macrorhiza	0	0			1	0	0	1									
Opuntia sp.	0	1			0	0	0	0									
Opuntia engelmannii	0	0			2	2	0	0									
Yucca madrensis	0	0			1	2	3	0									
Tree																	
Juniperus deppeana	0	0			0	0	0	0									
Pinus discolor	0	0			0	2	0	0									
Prosopis velutina	0	2			0	0	0	5									
Quercus arizonica	0	0			0	1	4	0									
Quercus emoryi	1	0			5	5	3	0									
Quercus oblongifolia	0	0			1	0	0	0									
Vine																	
Ipomoea coccinea	0	0			0	0	3	0									
Ipomoea longifolia	0	0			0	0	0	0									
Maurandella antirrhiniflora	0	0			0	0	3	0									
Phaseolus sp.	0	0			0	0	5	0									
Vitis arizonica	0	0			0	0	0	0									

Table B4a. Within-plot frequency (0–5) for all plots and species sampled on monitoring plots, low-elevation strata, Coronado NMEM, 2009–2010, cont.

| | 401 | | | | 402 | | | | | | | | | | | | |
| | 2009 | 2010 | 2011 | | 2009 | | 2010 | | 2011 | | | 2012 | | | 2013 | | |
Scientific name	401_V01	401_V02	401_V03	401_V04	402_V01	402_V02	402_V03	402_V04	402_V05	402_V06	402_V07	402_V08	402_V09	402_V10	402_V11	402_V12	402_V13
Not identified to species																	
Acourtia sp.	0	0			0	0	0	0									
Aster sp.	0	0			0	0	0	0									
Astrolepis sp.	0	0			0	0	0	0									
Bidens sp.	0	0			0	2	0	0									
Brassica sp.	0	0			0	0	0	0									
Chaenactis sp.	0	0			0	0	0	0									
Commelina sp.	0	0			0	0	0	0									
Cyperus sp.	0	0			2	5	0	0									
Datura sp.	0	0			0	1	0	0									
Erigeron sp.	4	3			5	3	0	5									
Eriogonum sp.	1	1			0	1	0	0									
Galium sp.	0	0			0	1	0	0									
Juncus sp.	0	0			0	0	0	0									
Macranthera sp.	0	0			0	0	3	0									
Notholaena sp.	0	0			0	0	5	0									
Pseudognaphalium sp.	0	0			0	0	0	4									
Rhus sp.	0	0			0	0	1	0									
Viguiera sp.	0	0			5	1	0	0									

Table B4b. Within-plot frequency (0–5) for all plots and species sampled on monitoring plots, high-elevation strata, Coronado NMEM, 2009–2010.

	502										503			
	2009		2010		2011		2012		2013		2009		2011	
Scientific name	502_V03	502_V04	502_V05	502_V08	502_V09	502_V10	502_V11	202_V12	502_V13	502_V14	503_V01	503_V06	503_V08	503_V09
Forb/Herb														
Ambrosia sp.	0	0	0	0							3	0		
Artemisia ludoviciana	1	2	5	3							3	5		
Bommeria hispida	0	0	2	0							1	2		
Castilleja tenuiflora	0	0	0	1							0	0		
Chamaesyce sp.	0	0	0	0							0	0		
Cheilanthes sp.	1	1	2	0							3	5		
Commelina erecta	0	1	0	0							0	0		
Conyza sp.	0	0	0	0							1	0		
Conyza canadensis	0	0	2	0							0	0		
Dalea sp.	0	0	2	0							0	1		
Evolvulus arizonicus	0	0	0	0							0	0		
Gnaphalium sp.	3	0	0	0							1	0		
Hedeoma dentata	0	1	0	0							4	0		
Hedeoma nana	0	0	5	1							0	5		
Ipomoea sp.	0	0	0	3							1	0		
Lasianthaea podocephala	0	0	0	0							0	0		
Machaeranthera tagetina	0	0	0	0							0	0		
Mirabilis longiflora	0	0	1	0							0	0		
ANNUAL FORB	3	2	2	1							3	0		
Najas marina	0	0	1	0							0	0		
Oenothera sp.	0	0	0	3							0	0		
Pellaea sp.	0	0	0	0							1	0		
Pellaea truncata	0	0	1	0							0	0		
Porophyllum ruderale	0	2	0	0							0	0		
Pseudognaphalium canescens	0	0	2	0							0	0		
Sida abutifolia	0	0	0	2							0	0		
Stachys coccinea	0	0	1	0							0	2		
Graminoid														
Aristida sp.	0	0	0	0							0	0		
Aristida purpurea	1	0	0	1							0	0		
Aristida schiedeana	5	2	5	1							5	5		
Aristida ternipes	4	1	3	0							4	1		
Bothriochloa barbinodis	2	5	3	4							1	1		
Bouteloua curtipendula	3	5	5	5							5	5		
Bouteloua gracilis	0	0	1	0							0	0		
Bouteloua hirsuta	5	1	1	0							2	5		
Bouteloua repens	4	0	3	0							0	0		
Bromus sp.	0	0	2	0							0	0		
Digitaria californica	0	0	3	0							0	0		

Table B4b. Within-plot frequency (0–5) for all plots and species sampled on monitoring plots, high-elevation strata, Coronado NMEM, 2009–2010, cont.

| | 502 | | | | | | | | | | 503 | | | |
| | 2009 | | 2010 | | 2011 | | 2012 | | 2013 | | 2009 | | 2011 | |
Scientific name	502_V03	502_V04	502_V05	502_V08	502_V09	502_V10	502_V11	202_V12	502_V13	502_V14	503_V01	503_V06	503_V08	503_V09
Graminoid, cont.														
Echinochloa sp.	0	0	1	0							1	0		
Elionurus barbiculmis	3	0	0	0							5	4		
Eragrostis intermedia	5	4	5	4							5	5		
Eragrostis lehmanniana	0	0	1	0							2	5		
Heteropogon contortus	0	0	0	0							1	2		
Leptochloa dubia	1	3	5	4							1	1		
Lycurus sp.	0	0	0	0							0	0		
Lycurus phleoides	0	2	0	0							0	0		
Lycurus setosus	5	5	5	4							0	3		
Muhlenbergia emersleyi	5	5	5	5							5	5		
Muhlenbergia polycaulis	0	0	0	1							0	0		
Muhlenbergia tenuifolia	0	0	1	0							0	0		
ANNUAL GRASS	0	3	0	0							0	0		
Schizachyrium sp.	5	0	3	0							3	5		
Schizachyrium cirratum	0	0	0	0							2	0		
Sporobolus wrightii	0	0	0	0							0	0		
Trachypogon spicatus	0	0	0	0							0	3		
Subshrub														
Acacia angustissima	4	3	4	0							5	1		
Bouvardia ternifolia	0	2	4	1							2	0		
Brickellia sp.	2	5	0	5							2	0		
Brickellia californica	0	0	5	0							1	5		
Brickellia venosa	0	4	0	0							0	0		
Dalea albiflora	0	0	0	0							1	0		
Desmodium cinerascens	0	0	0	0							0	4		
Ericameria laricifolia	0	0	0	0							5	5		
Eriogonum wrightii	0	0	1	0							0	0		
Galium wrightii	0	0	0	0							3	0		
Geranium caespitosum	0	0	0	0							0	0		
Gymnosperma glutinosum	1	3	0	4							0	0		
Nolina microcarpa	1	4	0	3							0	0		
Solanum elaeagnifolium	1	0	0	0							0	0		
Trichostema arizonicum	4	1	0	0							5	4		
Viguiera cordifolia	0	0	1	0							0	0		
Xanthisma spinulosum	0	0	0	0							0	0		

Table B4b. Within-plot frequency (0–5) for all plots and species sampled on monitoring plots, high-elevation strata, Coronado NMEM, 2009–2010, cont.

	502										503			
	2009		2010		2011		2012		2013		2009		2011	
Scientific name	502_V03	502_V04	502_V05	502_V08	502_V09	502_V10	502_V11	202_V12	502_V13	502_V14	503_V01	503_V06	503_V08	503_V09
Shrub														
Aloysia wrightii	0	2	0	0							0	0		
Arctostaphylos pungens	0	0	0	0							0	0		
Baccharis sp.	0	0	0	0							0	0		
Baccharis pteronioides	1	0	3	1							0	1		
Baccharis sarothroides	0	0	0	0							0	0		
Calliandra eriophylla	0	0	0	0							0	0		
Calliandra humilis	0	0	0	0							0	0		
Cercocarpus montanus	0	2	4	5							0	0		
Garrya wrightii	0	3	0	5							0	0		
Mimosa aculeaticarpa	0	0	1	1							1	0		
SNAG	4	5	4	5							5	5		
Rhus trilobata	0	0	0	1							0	0		
Rhus virens	1	1	2	5							0	1		
Rhus virens var. choriophylla	0	1	0	0							0	0		
Succulent														
Agave palmeri	0	1	1	1							5	1		
Agave parryi	0	0	1	0							0	0		
Cylindropuntia acanthocarpa	0	0	0	0							0	0		
Cylindropuntia leptocaulis	0	0	0	0							0	0		
Cylindropuntia spinosior	0	5	2	2							1	1		
Cylindropuntia versicolor	0	0	0	0							0	0		
Dasylirion wheeleri	5	5	5	5							5	5		
Echinocereus pectinatus	0	1	0	0							3	1		
Jatropha macrorhiza	0	0	0	0							0	0		
Opuntia sp.	0	0	0	0							0	1		
Opuntia engelmannii	0	1	0	0							3	0		
Yucca madrensis	1	1	4	2							2	3		
Tree														
Juniperus deppeana	4	1	0	1							0	0		
Pinus discolor	2	0	0	0							2	1		
Prosopis velutina	0	0	0	0							0	0		
Quercus arizonica	0	0	2	0							0	1		
Quercus emoryi	5	3	3	0							4	5		
Quercus oblongifolia	0	0	0	0							0	0		
Vine														
Ipomoea coccinea	0	0	4	1							0	0		
Ipomoea longifolia	0	0	4	0							0	0		
Maurandella antirrhiniflora	0	0	0	0							0	0		
Phaseolus sp.	0	0	0	0							0	4		
Vitis arizonica	0	0	0	1							0	0		

Table B4b. Within-plot frequency (0–5) for all plots and species sampled on monitoring plots, high-elevation strata, Coronado NMEM, 2009–2010, cont.

	502										503			
	2009		2010		2011		2012		2013		2009		2011	
Scientific name	502_V03	502_V04	502_V05	502_V08	502_V09	502_V10	502_V11	202_V12	502_V13	502_V14	503_V01	503_V06	503_V08	503_V09
Not identified to species														
Acourtia sp.	0	0	0	0							0	5		
Aster sp.	2	0	0	0							0	0		
Astrolepis sp.	0	0	0	0							0	2		
Bidens sp.	0	0	0	0							0	0		
Brassica sp.	0	0	0	1							0	0		
Chaenactis sp.	0	0	0	1							0	0		
Commelina sp.	2	0	1	0							4	1		
Cyperus sp.	0	0	0	0							2	3		
Datura sp.	0	0	0	0							0	0		
Erigeron sp.	0	0	0	0							2	2		
Eriogonum sp.	0	0	1	0							0	0		
Galium sp.	0	0	0	0							0	0		
Juncus sp.	0	0	0	0							1	0		
Macranthera sp.	0	0	0	0							1	0		
Notholaena sp.	0	0	2	0							0	0		
Pseudognaphalium sp.	0	0	0	0							0	0		
Rhus sp.	0	0	0	0							0	0		
Viguiera sp.	4	5	5	5							5	5		

Table B5a. Soil substrate (% by class) and surface aggregate stability class (mean and SE) and proportion of samples in "very stable" (=6) category, by monitoring plot, low-elevation strata, Coronado NMEM, 2009–2010.

| | 401 | | | | 402 | | | | | | | | | | | | |
| | 2009 | 2010 | 2011 | | 2009 | | 2010 | | 2011 | | | 2012 | | | 2013 | | |
Parameter	401_V01	401_V02	401_V03	401_V04	402_V01	402_V02	402_V03	402_V04	402_V05	402_V06	402_V07	402_V08	402_V09	402_V10	402_V11	402_V12	402_V13
Substrate																	
Bare soil (<2 mm), no overhead cover	0%	0%			0%	0%	1%	0%									
Bare soil (<2 mm), under vegetation	6%	19%			1%	2%	12%	28%									
Light cyanobacteria	0%	2%			0%	0%	0%	1%									
Litter and duff (organic matter)	71%	67%			72%	82%	59%	53%									
Dark cyanobacteria	0%	2%			0%	0%	0%	1%									
Gravel (2–75 mm)	5%	0%			20%	1%	4%	4%									
Lichen	0%	0%			0%	0%	0%	0%									
Moss	0%	0%			0%	0%	0%	0%									
Rock (76–600 mm)	0%	0%			0%	10%	8%	0%									
Lichen on rock	0%	0%			0%	0%	0%	0%									
Plant base	18%	10%			7%	5%	13%	13%									
Bedrock	0%	0%			0%	0%	3%	0%									
Surface Soil Aggregate Stability																	
Under vegetation																	
Average soil stability	4.09	5.46			4.80	5.08	4.10	5.05									
SD	1.99	0.68			1.65	1.74	2.14	1.20									
SE	0.29	0.10			0.30	0.34	0.39	0.19									
% samples "very stable"	37%	56%			50%	69%	43%	51%									
n	46	48			30	26	30	41									
No vegetation cover																	
Average soil stability	1.00	---			1.00	5.00	2.25	---									
SD	n/a	---			n/a	n/a	1.89	---									
SE	n/a	---			n/a	n/a	0.95	---									
% samples "very stable"	0%	---			0%	0%	0%	---									
n	1	0			1	1	4	0									

Decreasing erosion hazard (vertical axis label adjacent to Substrate rows)

Table B5b. Soil substrate (% by class) and surface aggregate stability class (mean and SE) and proportion of samples in "very stable" (=6) category, by monitoring plot, high-elevation strata, Coronado NMEM, 2009–2010.

Parameter	502 2009 502_V03	502 2009 502_V04	502 2010 502_V05	502 2010 502_V08	502 2011 502_V09	502 2011 502_V10	502 2012 202_V11	502 2012 202_V12	502 2013 502_V13	502 2013 502_V14	503 2009 503_V01	503 2009 503_V06	503 2011 503_V08	503 2011 503_V09
Substrate														
Bare soil (<2 mm), no overhead cover	1%	2%	1%	2%							0%	3%		
Bare soil (<2 mm), under vegetation	3%	6%	5%	19%							8%	5%		
Light cyanobacteria	0%	0%	0%	0%							0%	0%		
Litter and duff (organic matter)	36%	16%	38%	27%							42%	52%		
Dark cyanobacteria	0%	0%	0%	0%							0%	0%		
Gravel (2–75 mm)	16%	45%	20%	25%							21%	5%		
Lichen	0%	0%	0%	0%							0%	0%		
Moss	0%	0%	0%	0%							0%	0%		
Rock (76–600 mm)	17%	8%	8%	2%							15%	25%		
Lichen on rock	0%	0%	7%	2%							0%	2%		
Plant base	21%	15%	10%	14%							9%	8%		
Bedrock	6%	9%	10%	9%							4%	0%		
Surface Soil Aggregate Stability														
Under vegetation														
Average soil stability	5.53	3.97	5.06	4.60							3.69	3.85		
SD	0.99	1.70	1.30	1.68							2.22	2.09		
SE	0.17	0.31	0.22	0.28							0.39	0.40		
% samples "very stable"	71%	26%	46%	43%							34%	33%		
n	34	31	35	35							32	27		
No vegetation cover														
Average soil stability	4.29	2.67	4.00	1.50							3.60	3.56		
SD	1.80	1.633	1.60	1.069							2.41	2.24		
SE	0.68	0.67	0.57	0.38							1.08	0.75		
% samples "very stable"	29%	0%	13%	0%							20%	33%		
n	7	6	8	8							5	9		

Decreasing erosion hazard →